REDNECK ECONOMICS

REDNECK ECONOMICS

John W. Terry

iUniverse, Inc.
New York Lincoln Shanghai

REDNECK ECONOMICS

iUniverse, Inc.

For information address:
iUniverse, Inc.
2021 Pine Lake Road, Suite 100
Lincoln, NE 68512
www.iuniverse.com

ISBN: 0-595-32832-6

Printed in the United States of America

A special thanks to my Uncle's "Black", Claude Thurman, "Bunyan", Paul Baird; even though they may not agree with some of my opinions they were the inspiration.

Also thank you to my parents, Auston & Judy Terry, to Kevin Dahl, and Ms. Soojin Yoon.

John Terry
31 July 2004

Contents

1

YOU CAN'T MAKE CHICKEN SALAD OUT OF CHICKEN SHIT

The substance of this work is solid fundamentals, hence the underlying meaning of this chapter. This book does not consist of any complicated formulas of how to make money, (if I new one I damn sure wouldn't put it here, nor would anyone else they'd use it themselves). Sorry I don't know any get rich schemes; unless you can throw a baseball 100 MPH your doomed like most of us to a life of hard work. This book is to help set a guideline for ones financial, economic and hopefully political ideas. Warning for those extreme left liberals (communist bastards), you may take offense to my Classical Liberalism (the true liberals) or ridicule it, but to that I say look at your pay check. Do you really think big brother can manage your money better than you? Look at how much goes to Social Security, then look at projections of when Social Security will be broke, gee do you think you'll get your money back? Maybe congress should change the name to Social Insecurity.

What led me to writing this were many long conversations with my Uncle Black sitting on his porch, getting drunk and solving the world's problems. And by God we solved them, but nobody listened. As a matter of fact the title of this chapter came from one of Black's schemes (stories) he had for making some money.

Making chicken salad out of chicken shit. Now before you decide to ask for the garden salad, this is not a direct process, so don't puke your guts out just yet, (although sometimes salad has a, how should I say this, well a cleansing effect on my digestive track).

First off in order to create chicken shit you need some goddamn chickens so first off go out and get some diddles. Now while the diddles are reaching maturity (got to have full blown chicken shit) dig yourself a big ass pond and fill it full of carp. Now here's the key, carp will eat damn nye anything, so feed the Sons of Bitches the chicken shit. You will have to sell the chicken eggs to buy a tractor trailer truck with a refer (for you potheads a refer in this case is a refrigerated trailer) so you can harvest some of the carp, take them down to a big city and sell them to the less fortunate. You take the money made off the carp to buy some more diddles. If your fortunate enough to have property in East Tennessee you can gather up some Poke salad cull out a few old chickens, slice, dice, grill, mix up and wallah! Take that shit to the Yuppie health nuts in the Ritzy part of that same big city and charge a huge price for your all-natural, purely organic chicken salad.

I also felt a duty to my beliefs to try and get peoples attention to how far this country has drifted from the views of our founding fathers, the laissez-faire economics and sound thrift that made this country the best land on the planet. And no these aren't the views of some rich kid born with a silver spoon in his mouth and nothing to do but take erotic drugs and sit around philosophizing all day. I was raised in Ohio by two Briar Hopping Hillbillies from East Tennessee. My mom was the perfect definition of the Coal Miners Daughter and Dad spent his younger days eating the dust of an old mule and working in the logwoods.

Although I think the world of my parents I do not share their political views, since they are both strong Democrats. I can understand why a working class person would be a Democrat, since they give the appearance of doing something for the poor, but their social programs undermine the very fabric of what the working class stands for, a strong work ethic. And by the way the Republicans are no better, their heading in the same direction as the Democrats going 50 MPH toward Socialism while the Donkeys blister away at 100 MPH.

Now that I've voiced some purpose, beliefs, and dislikes lets delve into some more dislikes. I cannot stand these Keynesians, Post-Keynesians, Neo-Keynesians, or whatever labels these growth in government advocates are slapping themselves with. For one thing these so-called Keynesians need to go back and read what the man (John Maynard Keynes) actually wrote. Keynes advocated setting up a government investment fund, with an educated elite group of members deciding on what industries to develop with these public funds. The money was to come from a tax collected during strong economic times then used during an economic downturn. But politicians only saw the ability to assure the public that the government would do something during a recession, namely run up big deficits and the threat of inflation. As a matter of fact near the end of WWII when it was apparent the allies were on the road to victory they held an economic summit in Bretton Woods, New Hampshire in July of 1944. Plenty of prominent businessmen, politicians and policy makers were in attendance, including Lord Keynes himself. Thanks to this meeting of the minds we have such fiscally irresponsible and sovereignty stealing institutions as the ITO (International Trade Organization) now the WTO (World Trade Organization) by way of GATT (General Agreement on Tariffs and Trade), the IMF (International Monetary Fund) and the mother fucking United Nations. Ironically when this meeting concluded which supposedly embrace the ideas of Keynes, he announced that he was the only non-Keynsian there. Now don't get me wrong I damn sure ain't recommending a true Keynesian economic policy (although it would be an improvement over this deficit building). I don't need some spoiled rotten, filthy rich Ivy-League grad sitting in a think tank within the District of Columbia deciding how I should spend my money. I figure John Q. Public (The Consumer) can inform business what to invest in better than some egg-headed philosopher in Washington.

Now that you have an inkling of my background and a bigger dose than you probably cared of some of my beliefs, I'll move on by giving you a brief description of the topics in the following chapters. In the first topic of the following chapter we are going to explore some sound fundamentals for a variety of topics that I deem relevant to this work (for example, long term investing, the importance of thrift, ect.). Yes I'm using the old model of building a house with a strong foundation, for here on Spaceship Earth us Dudley Dumbshits need discipline that can at least allow us to pick ourselves off the ground and get headed in the right direction, (note: for the rest of this book any time I refer to Dudley I'm encompassing Mr. Dumbshit and the uncanny ability of the human species to overlook the obvious and/or think he's figured out everything and fall flat on his face.). After that chapter 3 will expand upon our home to frame it in a way that it doesn't look like a lean-to; built by a pack of Cub-Scouts at their first summer camp. And this will be done by keeping it simple, no Pythagorean theorem or Fuzzy Math. From there its on to chapter 4 were you will be introduced to all you need to remember about economics. Some memorization skills are required but believe me even Dudley Dumbshit will remember these points for they are few and yes they are simple. Then we will attempt to take out the trash by throwing out some things we don't need to believe, namely the so-called experts. Next we'll get into some particulars of personal investment and affiliation. Finally we'll nail down the roof with some simple reasoning and matters of the heart; don't get excited, I'm no Casanova, these won't be exquisite one-liners for picking up a piece at the local bar.

Now you might be saying, hey dumbass what the hell does reasoning and personal feelings have to do with economics, well you brain washed Son of Bitch it has much to do about everything, not to be confused with Shakespeare's *Much to do About Nothing*. For economics is a social science and no matter how hard academia tries to make economics a hard science by introducing math, economics still comes down to individuals making decisions based on personal preferences (feelings). As Ludwig von Mises so eloquently stated, "No treatment of economic problems proper can avoid starting from acts of choice, economics becomes a part, although the hitherto best elaborated part, of a more universal science, praxeology". No matter how much those long-haired hippy type fags out in Cali-wierd wave peace symbols around while talking smack about big corporations and the wonders of living in harmony with the planet without worrying about money, every decision has financial consequences. Even if those queers decide to save 'valuable' rain forests by not wiping their ass with toilet paper that has economic ramifications. One, some poor aborigine just lost a months pay resulting in one of his little rug rats to starve to death, cause that hippy in Frisco wanted to know what his filthy ass would smell like not using some sinful capitalistic ass wipe, then of course the stupid Frisco hippy gets rotten crotch and his fag partner gets the ole drippy dick, and they both spend a war pension at the doctor all because they decided to save one rotten tree in a third world country but wound up destroying a whole forest with the money they wound up wasting.

2

SOUND FUNDAMENTALS

Chapter two is on Sound Fundamentals, or if you prefer making sure there's some meat in our salad and no chicken shit. We're going to need some solid techniques that we can build upon and also fall back on in tough times. These ideas must coincide with an overall purpose of improvement and enhancement. This chapter will cover building beliefs in our purpose then setting out to achieve the wanted goal. These topics will include goals, organization, career, investing, politics, intrinsic value, and a backup plan. I will use the baseball career of Barry Bonds as an example for introducing the topics in this chapter. Of course Bonds was born with exceptional talent but that does not completely explain his career, which began as a speedy leadoff hitter that developed into the most feared power hitter in the game. Now this didn't happen over night if you look at his early career numbers he rarely hit 20 homers let alone anything near seventy-three. He obviously set a goal of improving his physical ability (strength conditioning) and baseball mentality (pitch selection); these two goals are what I would label sub goals to his overall goal of becoming a better hitter. Once Mr. Bonds had established his goals, he invested time and money into achieving his aim of becoming a more complete baseball player. He invested time in physical conditioning. He spent money on personal trainers and dieticians. Some players even invested money in "enhancers" to improve their strength, now I am not saying Barry Bonds is one of those players. Mr. Bonds has also done some pretty good politicking to make himself a tad bit more famous along the way, (or infamous). By this I don't mean he has been out electioneering for office, and he might not even realize that he's playing the politics of the baseball media, he is more likely just being himself. But when he acts like an ass towards the media and makes some outlandish comments about Babe Ruth, well quite frankly he's done a damn fine job of drawing even more attention to himself. Bonds seems to have created an aura about him that distances himself from others creating an atmosphere that he's unapproachable, making him more of a mystery, and a better story. Next topic regarding Mr. Bonds would be intrinsic value, well hell he's a baseball player, not many things have more intrinsic value than the game of baseball (if you couldn't tell baseball is my favorite sport). And the final topical comparison is the backup plan, he's filthy freaking rich, so what the hell!

The most important idea to everyone is of course to maximize happiness. Everyone has different likes and dislikes; and thankfully so or we would all be stepping in chicken shit looking for the chicken salad. Sounds simple enough, do what makes us happy, but what makes us happy may create a disaster tomorrow and that is not maximizing your happiness. For example New Years Eve party, New Years Day hangover. Also one has to consider their talents and find out what they do best. I was a decent High School baseball player but at 6 feet tall a buck forty and a fastball topping out at 75 MPH, Dudley wasn't going to be making a living toeing the rubber at Yankee Stadium.

So an important aspect of moving toward our greater well-being and happiness is to set goals. Now this doesn't necessarily have to be geared to financial success, although it sounds like a good one to me. Money might not buy happiness but it makes a damn good placebo. Of course its great to set family and career goals, and one might keep a personal view to helping his fellow man. The important thing when setting a goal I believe is setting the goal with the aim of making a difference. Goals help give a sense of direction and when surpassed a feeling of accomplishment and drive to attain more.

Once we have found what we like and determined some goals we need some organization. If things are not organized you'll windup heading the wrong direction, and backtracking to get headed down the right path. Organization minimizes frustration, now it does not eliminate it but it helps even during a setback to get pointed (or keep us pointed) in the right direction. This helps us maximize our time thereby increasing our accomplishments. "Don't agonize. Organize." (Florence Kennedy)

These fundamentals must be applied to a career and life plan. One should naturally pick the career that brings them the most happiness. Now I'm not talking about just the on the job happiness. You must look at the overall picture, who the hell wants to get up and go to work anyway. But if you do live and breath your work, well that's just out-fucking standing, I'm happy for you, but I never saw a tombstone that read I wish I would have worked more. And that crap about my job doesn't challenge me. Hell if you're that gung ho, challenge yourself, do some self-enhancing in your free time (school, hobby) or better yet start your own business.

The most important life plan and career fundamental is education. Education can be broken down into two types; 1: personal 'enrichment' like learning the guitar; 2: personal 'en*rich*ment' taking a Finance 101 class. Ones education does not have to solely be formal classroom training. If we have a goal and plan learning becomes more enjoyable since it adds purpose to the learning. Also your education does not have to be completely geared toward your career. Education of some form should be a priority and an ongoing goal, once a desired level is reached in a particular subject decide whether to strive for a higher level or move to a different subject. Learning other skills or hobbies add to your personal fulfillment and you might happen to find something else you're good at and/or enjoy.

Another important aspect is investing, we must be able to fund our plans or the attainment of the goal is lost, unless your goal is to die empty-handed, but we know the only rule to the game of life is; he who dies with the most toys wins. I am not going to go into any great detail about investing as that is reserved to a later chapter. But I will mention a few of the more important ideas. One is diversification sometimes referred to as deworseification but unless you're lucky it's a pretty damn good idea. Another is to have a long-range mentality, of course Lord Keynes pointed out so poetically that in the long-run we're all dead. But what the hell we can hope maybe someone will find a cure for the aging process and we will live forever. On second thought scratch that, who the hell wants to spend eternity here, especially for those unfortunate fools who are married, talk about damned for eternity. Something to avoid in the world of investing is speculation, and by having that long-run mentality we can help to avoid this disastrous scheme. Keep in mind what legendary financial mind Benjamin Graham said, "Outright speculation is neither illegal, immoral, nor (for most people) fattening to the pocket book."

"Politicians"; need I say more, oh but I will, rotten no good scoundrels, scum of the earth, but keep in mind these pricks are making the laws of the land. More importantly they decide what to do with our hard earned cash. So remember at the voting booth, unless you're on welfare every vote for larger government (food for thought, government is the most inefficient institution known to man, remember government does not create jack shit, but its damn good at destroying) is a vote to remove money from your pocket.

Intrinsic value is an important concept that one should keep in mind when making any important decision. Intrinsic value meaning something is good in and of itself. For example money itself is worthless but food and water are essentials to survival. Property (a home) has intrinsic value, hell you have to have a place to roost, plus land can provide food. An essential lesson of intrinsic value is to make sure you do not build a house of cards. Keep in mind basic assets that insure survival and a comfortable living.

Look toward and be confident of victory, but don't get cocky and keep in mind defeat and a line of retreat. In other words have a backup plan. Yes shit happens and if you don't have a backup plan you might be tempted to commit suicide and self-destruction is not an adequate backup plan. P.S. a good backup plan is moving back in with your parents.

So we have the chicken by the back of the neck fixin to ring him up and add some meat to our salad, lets remember the fundamentals. One, do what you do best and have fun, shit that sounds easy enough. ORGANIZE, SET GOALS, advance, next. Financially live within your means. Politically do what's best for you the consumer/investor and its probably the best for the nation, ("Every individual necessarily labors to render the annual revenue of the society as great as he can. He generally indeed neither intends to promote the public interest, nor knows how much he is promoting it. He intends only his own gain, and he is in this, as in many other cases, led by an invisible hand to promote an end which was no part of his intention. By pursuing his own interest he frequently promotes that of the society more effectually than when he really intends to promote it. I have never known much good done by those who affected to trade for the public good." Adam Smith). Keep in mind intrinsic value it may keep you from reverting to the backup plan.

Now that we've carved up the chicken into some sound ideas its time to grab that head of lettuce and make a real salad by keeping it simple stupid.

3

K.I.S.S. THEORY

K.I.S.S. = Keep It Simple Stupid

"Don't try to do good, let good emerge as the by-product of selfishness."
Adam Smith

I can't think of a simpler life motto that that. As you should have gathered by now this chapter focuses on simplicity. It will give some very basic investment advice and also a piercing blitzkrieg of Government bureaucratic macro economic statistics.

When you get down to the nitty gritty this chapter is about tidying things up and taking out the garbage.

As noted earlier there's a whole chapter devoted to some specifics in investing, but some general direction will be given here. First of all the hardest part to any investment strategy is just getting started, just like old not so reliable parked out by the curb, once it cranks you breath a sigh of relief. Now once we've grabbed the bull by the horns we've gotta hold on and hopefully much longer than 8 seconds, for investing (saving) needs a long-range mentality and has to become routine. Its kind of like brushing your teeth, it has to become habit, but a good habit or put another way for this routine of investing you want to make sure its like getting a piece of ass and not like smoking crack, it has to go to something beneficial not destructive.

This routine needs a plan from day one, but like the Constitution, open to change. And also like the Constitution it shouldn't be easily changed, (although maybe our forefathers should have made it more difficult considering what those pricks on The Hill have done to it, but that's another matter). If you are constantly changing the plan, your going to be like a car stuck in a cesspool; constantly spinning your wheels, getting nowhere, and covered in shit. This plan needs to be long-term with an eye towards retirement. It should also include major purchases, everyday expenses, emergency funds, (yes unfortunately Shit Happens), and of course fun (need to raise some cain ever now and then). Next thing to remember, do not fall for those get rich quick schemes or some Ivy League Grad with a complicated formula. Now if playing hardball with Mr. Market using those complicated formula's gets your rocks off, well Dudley, have at it. Just keep in mind the possibility of side affects, for example migraines and a smaller bank account. In this plan to make it routine several avenues can be taken to help acquire the habit. Direct deposit or allotments to investment accounts are the best routine (well fuck their easy) hell they come straight out of your check, thereby bypassing the temptation to spend the money elsewhere. If your not wired for the technology age, try a calendar, putting in dates to write checks or make deposits or the old shoe-box with the thought of not touching it till the means to acquire the intended ends are met, of course this requires much more discipline. Now some advice nobody wants to here but it is the best way in the world to make more money, guaranteed, "CUT EXPENSES", of course us Dudley Dumbshits don't want to hear that little piece of wisdom. Nobody wants to take this step but it always works without fail. When it comes to investing keep in mind the simplicities of habitual routine and saving.

Another aspect of the KISS Theory involves avoidance, for example, not adding to your expenses without adding to your income by a greater amount. Avoid following the masses on Macro economic reports, their like lemmings headed toward the sea. Keeping track of the economy is fine, (I can't think of a safer sleeping pill than reading economic reports), but do not let daily recordings of economic statistics determine your investment decisions. Allowing daily reports to influence your finances leads to increased movements of assets, hence increased costs and worse yet may lead to an attempt at market timing. Now lets think about this "Market Timing", Mr. Market was here long before any of us Dudleys were even hatched and he will be here long after we become worm bait, so remember, time don't mean Jack Shit to Mr. Market.

There are many reasons to not put much faith in Macro Economic data, but number one on the list is most are put out by the government (need I say more). I'm thinking of starting a petition to have sent to congress that requires the consolidation of all statistical data into one agency called, Bureau of Statistics, at least that way the acronym would be correct "BS". A large number of statistics use a complicated formula or data collection process leaving too much room for error.

The following is a "simple" example of one of those macro economic statistics put out by your government:

Data source

- The PPI sample includes approximately 25,000 establishments providing close to 100,000 price quotations per month.

- Participating establishments report price data primarily through the mail.

- Goods and services included in the PPI are weighted by value-of-shipments data contained in the 1992 economic censuses.

- Industries and products are systematically resampled as needed.

Index calculation

In concept, the Producer Price Index is calculated according to a modified Laspeyres formula:

$$I_i = \left(\Sigma Q_a P_i / \Sigma Q_a P_o \right) \times 100$$

where:

P_o is the price of a commodity in the comparison period;

P_i is its price currently; and

Qa represents the quantity shipped during the weight-base period.

An alternative formula more closely approximates the actual computation procedure:

$$I_i = \left[\left(\Sigma Q_a P_o (P_i / P_o) \right) / \Sigma Q_a P_o \right] \times 100$$

In this form, the index is the weighted average of price relatives, i.e., price ratios for each item (P_i/P_o). The expression ($Q_a P_o$) represents the weights in value form, and the P and Q elements (both of which originally relate to period "a" but are adjusted for price change to period "o") are not derived separately. When specifications or samples change, the item relatives must be computed by linking (multiplying) the relatives for the separate periods for which the data are precisely comparable.

And believe it or not there is more detail to go along with the collection and calculation of this "simple" index at www.bls.gov just start clicking on anything that references the PPI. The math involved for calculating this index is rather simple despite all that damn Greek used in the formula. Once it's broken down and written out in real numbers its fairly straight forward for anyone who's had basic college math. But even this simple index calculation is made more complex by the fact that some of the data entered into the calculation is manipulated (supposedly to make it more accurate) through other voodoo like reweighting, date rebasement, hedonic modeling, and sometimes its just flat-out has bogus information entered in. Now the PPI has its flaws but at least it's not a complete waste of taxpayer money (the crooked goons on Wall Street and at the Fed plug it into their economic models). But another indicator (indicator of what who knows) the Import and Export Price Index, well, who the hell uses that? Now go grab a bunch of econ textbooks and do a walk thru their glossaries and indexes to see how many mention this program and you'll be hard pressed to find one if any. In a nutshell the Import and Export Price Index takes a sample of about 10,000 individual export items and 12,000 import items through questionnaires. What a waste of resources, especially when you consider what a small part the Gross Domestic Product is derived from net exports. GDP is calculated by the following formula: $Y = C+I+G+NX$. Were Y = GDP, C = Consumption, I = Investment, G = Government purchases, and NX = Net exports. And within this formula net exports is by far the smallest portion.

It just fucking amazes me that people think that all the economic activity of a nation can be accurately measured by a mathematical formula put out by a bunch of bureaucrats. The only thing measured by this is that the bureaucrats gain more appropriations from congressman who line their pockets by using this bullshit to get their programs (taxes) passed.

Now I will concede that once you have a formula computers make the actual calculation pretty simple, since computers are not human they don't screw up, of course 'minor glitches' still occur (CPI summer 2000), oh shit I forgot computers were invented by man, and I have yet to meet a flawless human (although I've looked at many pics of Brittney Spears and I ain't found a damn thing wrong with her, but I ain't met her in person). Well now lets move onto the collection of that data, talk about a grab bag. Some of this data is dependant upon voluntary information from the good faith of people who get no direct (or in my opinion indirect) benefit from this data. Talk about a crapshoot. Think about it, Uncle Sucker sends you a survey form on a routine basis that takes up your time, pays you nothing, hell actually your paying to do this, with at best minimal benefit to you. Ah shit Dudley how much effort would you put into this situation, except for those ignorant numbskulls that think government laid the golden egg, (fools, to lay an egg a chicken needs screwed, the only thing government ever screwed was the tax payers). To make matters worse these surveys are easily pencil whipped, for example a survey that asks for a price can easily be marked with an "X" for no change, giving the respondent who is probably actually busy doing real work that they earn money for a quick response to these surveys. And I'm not just guessing at this, I have worked on one of these surveys, its simply amazing how many things never change in a world with only one constant and that is change. Well it ain't hard to figure out that no matter how good one of these models are, if you feed it shit, Hallelujah, you get shit in return. I know some will say that some statistics have a "well tested" formula and that some agencies collect their own data avoiding these errors. Hmmmm… Well Einstein, it's still administered by humans and of all the great citizens of this country I have known and read about only two approached perfection, Robert E. Lee and George Washington. Lets see; Lee sent 15,000 troops into the center of the Union Lines at Gettysburg and Washington played in the rain and caught a chill and died, so even they fucked up.

Moving on, let us suppose that everyone associated with these economic models was able to walk on water and never make a mistake. That the data they collected was flawless. HOLY SHIT! By the grace of god the free world is saved! The numbers don't lie! The model spits out an absolute perfect picture of what WAS. Yes this is a perfect model of what has already happened. Hey Dudley, how the hell am I supposed to use this information? Yeah, this information is about as useful as tits on a boar hog. Don't worry the government had the answer way back in the early 20th century. Yes in 1913 these United States created the Federal Reserve. That all omniscient financial institution created because of some short financial panics (and for the most part localized), the most recent being 1907. Damn even when our government was relatively small and nimble it still took 6 years to answer the call. And just in time, the banking industry had already recovered, we were well on our way to world supremacy and the roaring twenty's. But thank god the Fed was there to correct the crash of 1929. Lets see prior to this little episode depressions were just that, depressions. Now we have the "Great Depression", but I tend to agree with my Uncle Paul who lived during the Great Depression, "I didn't see anything so great about it". Oh, I'm sorry, forgive me, it was the gold problem, since it was the backing of financial transactions between countries that tied the hands of the central Fed. Let me get this straight, the institution of gold, which had been around since before Christ had more bugs in it than one created 16 years before the Crash of 29, can I sell you some swamp land, Uncle Sam did.

If macro economic data is of some importance to the private enterprise, and I don't dispute that some are, well why the hell should some hermit it Wyoming have to pay for it. If it benefits someone they'll produce it at a profit, in a competitive market and much more efficiently than some damn bureaucracy, and despite these government reports some private agencies do provide this information, like Salomon Smith Barney reports, Wall Street Journal, and the financial markets themselves are good economic indicators (the DOW, S&P 500) But for the purpose of individual investing macro economic reports of any kind are of little use and for government economic policy their just plain wasteful. The jist of most of these statistics is to get a gauge on the direction and magnitude of the change in the overall economy. Why is a complicated economic model needed for guessing, and I do mean guessing what is happening to the economy. Think about it, any Dudley on the face of the planet with absolutely no data of any kind has a 1 in 3 chance of getting the direction right, (its either up, down, or no change). As for the magnitude, what difference does it make given the inherent flaws pointed out earlier in collecting and calculating macro economic data. I have serious doubts about the correctness in gauging the magnitude in macro economic data.

So, Keep It Simple Stupid (KISS). Make investing routine and as painless as possible, one more plug for those direct deposits and allotments, (if it ain't available you can't blow it). And for crying out loud avoid the Dung Pile, stay away from the bullshit that keeps you tuned into daily management of your portfolio, it becomes daily mistakes not management. Scrutinizing your money on a daily basis leads to more transactions, which results in more costs you have to recover just to brake even.

4

THINGS TO REMEMBER ABOUT ECONOMICS
(And Some to Forget)

Supply and Demand (S&D).

That's it, that's all you need to know about economics. Forget all those graphs that make you feel as though you enrolled in a Mandarin Chinese language class. No need to memorize any elaborate formulas, (I did this my college days, hell all you do is regurgitate it on some exam and forget it).

Having stated the above I am going to move on anyhow. I will go into some players and ideas that radiate from the wonders of S & D. Of the aforementioned Mr. Market comes into mind, for everything must be paid for in one way or another. The creation of Mr. Market stems from the need to allocate scarce resources with the least amount of waste, and the drive to accomplish is benefited greatly by mans greed. And these factors will always remain, the talk of a "new economy" is utter nonsense, the laws of economics apply equally to all products, there may be new products replacing old, but this does not change the actors or the natural law of the markets.

Supply and Demand. Now who knows the laws of S & D better than anyone else, why of course Mr. Market, although some people, politicians, policy makers and some dumbass economists say they understand these laws (hint don't believe them). The old adage that there is no free lunch is an absolute. Everything must be paid for in some way. Now as I softly referred to in the previous chapter, don't play hardball with Mr. Market, he always wins, even if you win he does too, remember he will be here when your bones are transformed into coal, and sold on the market.

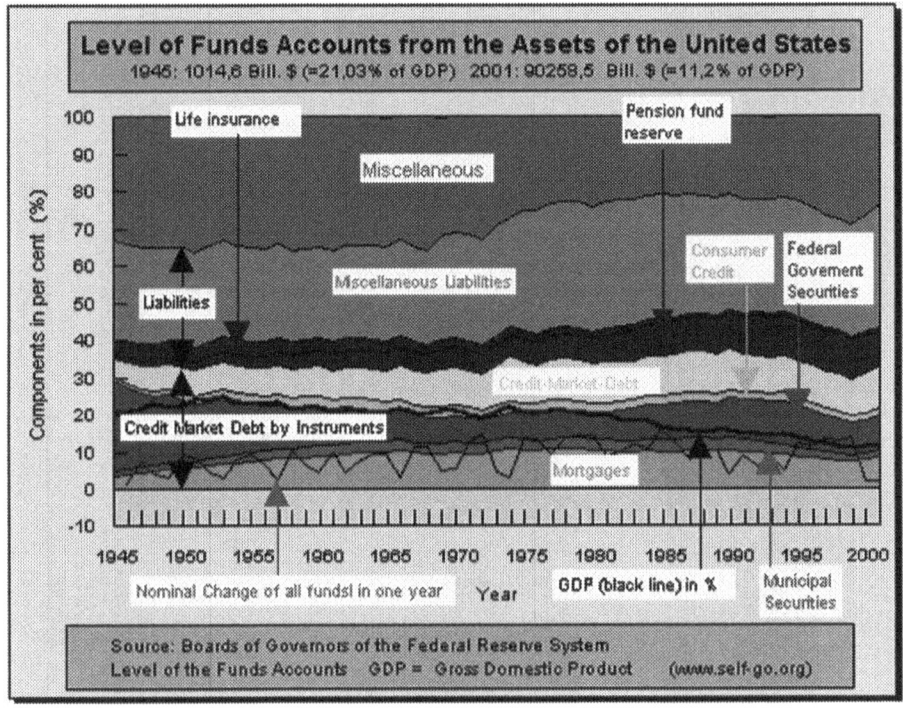

(Fig. 4-1)

What the fuck is this? Compare this shit to figure 4-2.

Note: this graph was compiled using Federal Reserve data and can be found on the Internet at www.self-go.org. This is actually a very good site with some strong libertarian ideas.

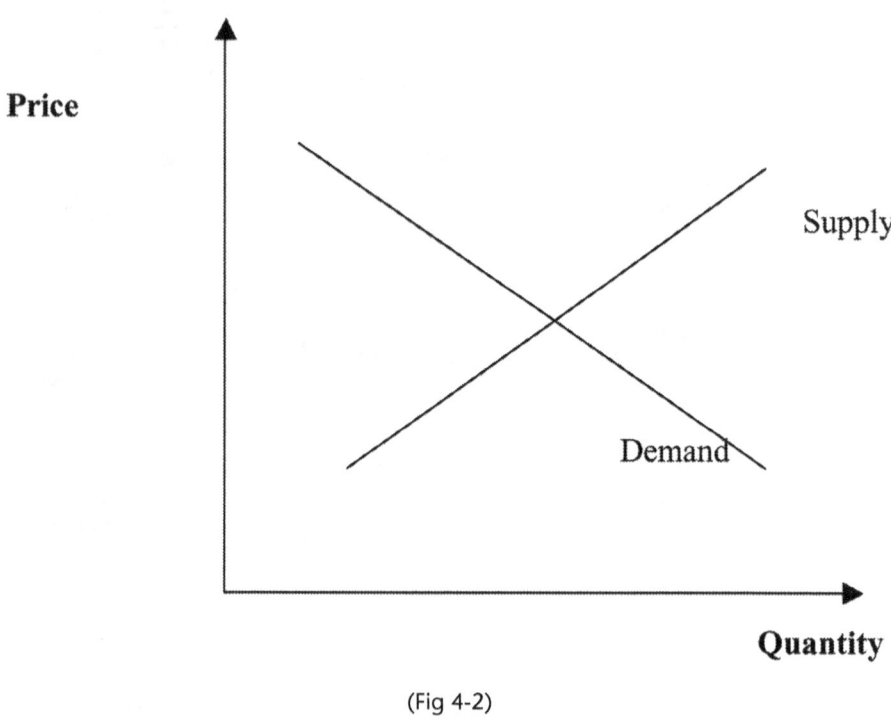

(Fig 4-2)

All you need to know about economics explained in this simple graph. Were demand equals supply will determine the quantity produced and the price paid.

Kings, Queens, Emperors, Presidents, and Philosophers have all tried to modify or eliminate Mr. Market, but with the power of Supply and Demand and Father time on his side he always opens great big can of wup ass.

From 1542-1551 King Henry VIII of England took an old government trick to new extremes. The idea is known as debasement, which is when the government lessens the value of the metal content in its coins (in this case silver). When Henry started his Hanky Panky the silver content in a pound sterling was 6.4 troy ounces, but he managed to whittle that down to 1.2 troy ounces when all was said and done. Good ole Hank wanted to pay for his welfare warfare state by stealing his subjects' silver. Of course this caused the mints to work over time stamping out the ever more worthless coins which of course created rampant inflation, especially in grain prices. Naturally this brought on Gresham's Law; the idea that bad money drives out good money, which in this case specifically means the populous finally got wise to the thieves trick and melted down the older "good coins" for their silver content and used the newer "bad coins" to pay off their debts, which naturally pissed off the merchants causing them to refuse the newer coins even though the coins were legal tender. As a result Hank had to exert more centralized control of power, expansion of Middle Age serfdom and prolonged misery for all of mankind, thanks your heinous.

But you say; Mr. Dudley Dumbshit in modern America we don't have kings, we have democratically elected Presidents. Well fartknocker, I hate to burst your bubble but we still windup with leaders like Richard Millhouse (Tricky Dick) Nixon whom think they can control Mr. Market. In the early seventies inflation started to rear its ugly head. President Nixon decided to implement price controls by setting a ceiling on a broad range of products. Naturally this lead to shortages since producers can't bring goods to the market if they're not able to cover their cost (i.e. labor). Price controls seem like a bad idea (and are a bad idea) but old Millhouse and his brilliant economic mind decided to do something in addition to this by completely dissolving the quasi-gold dollar standard of the Bretton Woods agreement. Of course foreign banks dumped the dollar flooding the market with the worthless paper causing gold to rise from the standard $35 an ounce in 1971 to $125 an ounce by 1973. Then Mr. Market jumped in with a devastating one-two punch, causing something economist at the time thought was impossible, increasing inflation with rising unemployment, and the birth of a beautiful new economic term; stagflation (good job Dick).

The omnipotent government has also spoke of evil monopolies created by the free market, but in the same forked tongue breath say certain monopolies must exist for the good of society, and of course the government decides which monopolies must be created. A good example of this government omnipotence or ineptness in this folly is the British governments creation of the South Sea Company in 1711. The Limy government had run up massive debt and they felt this monopoly was needed to restore faith in the English governments ability to pay its debts. They hoped to do this by giving the company a monopoly on all South Sea trade, and in exchange the company took on some of the government debt. Well back in the 1700's government action benefited the same goons it does today, the well established insiders.

STAGFLATION

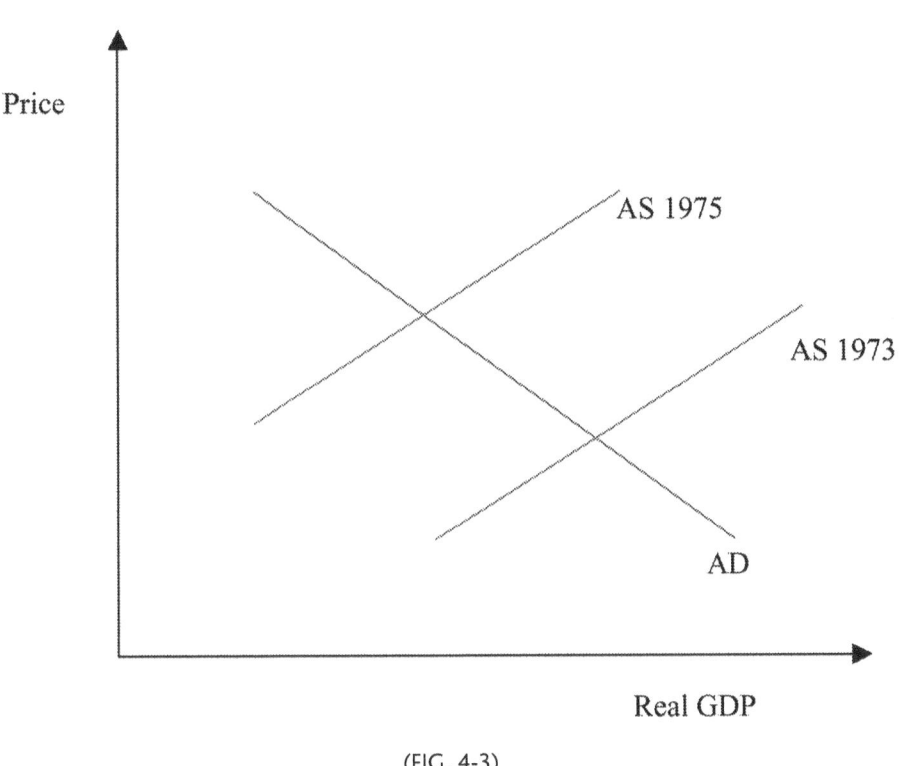

(FIG. 4-3)

AS = Aggregate Supply
AD = Aggregate Demand

Privileged individuals were able to buy the government debt for 55 pounds sterling and convert that into the stock of the South Sea Company, which was worth 100 pounds. Naturally the umbrella toting limy government set the company up with painstaking detail, and not a damn one of the officials picked to run the company knew jack squat about South Sea trade. If anyone would have bothered to check, the biggest revenue garnishing market in the area was the slave trade, but large revenue does not always translate into profit. The ships were so poorly equipped that most of the slaves died during the voyage. By god those pricks might not have been good traders but were outstanding con-artists. They rented a lavish house in London and put forth the look of righteous high-rollers. Author John Caswell wrote of John Blunt, one of the principle directors, "he continued to live his life with a prayer-book in his right hand and a prospectus in his left, never letting his right hand know what his left hand was doing." With elaborate concoctions of a booming gold and cotton trade from the Americas the stock in the company went to 300 pounds, then 550, and all the way to 1000 pounds sterling. Finally the yarn started to unravel. The company directors knowing damn good and well the stock was not worth the paper it was written on; sold out. When the news of who was selling leaked out, panic rained down, and the public confidence the government had originally tried to regain collapsed.

I have told about Mr. Market wuppin on a President and a King, now its time for Mr. Market to kick some Roman Emperor ass. In 293 A.D. Diocletian decided that the empire had grown to big to be effectively governed (which was probably true). His solution, create an even bigger bureaucracy to manage it. Diocletian setup four districts each governed by a Caesar (title not name), insisting all along the empire was still equal and undivided. Well someone should have thrown up a big bullshit flag, bureaucracies feed on themselves, their very nature is to grow bigger and gain more power and influence. As time went on the four districts naturally struggled for power, wearing Diocletian down, causing an extremely rare event, the voluntary abdication of a Roman Emperor. Diocletian threw in the towel and headed for the country (literally); while his son Constantine fled in fear of his life (the son would learn from his fathers mistakes as he later returned to become Constantine the Great, but another seed of destruction had already been sown). Now obviously this bonehead idea of Diocletians' didn't bring an end to the Roman Empire, but it sure didn't help, and I know this, no country on the planet uses Latin as its primary language anymore.

Next lets mention a profession that with little or no direct control of the subjects they come to influence, still manage to create as much damage using their brain (or lack thereof) as any armies brawn, philosophers. Since this subject could cover a whole book 100 times the size of this one, I will keep it narrowed down to a couple of fairly recent ones. Karl Marx, born in Germany; his ideas were so fucked up he had to leave the Fatherland for jolly old England, hell his ideas were rejected by the ultimate Kraut loving Austrian, Hitler. Of course the economic philosophy of this longhaired 19th century hippy is communism. On the surface communism sounds like a good idea to the little man, were the wealth of the nation is shared "equally". But that scraggly looking S.O.B. forgot one slight detail. Wheres the fucking incentive if everybody gets the same thing! Think of it this way, however small your wealth may be are you willing to give that up to share with the lazy fucks who have less than you? Communism by definition does not give bonuses for hard work; the commie creed goes something like this, "From each according to his abilities, to each according to his needs." Look at the great communist experiment, the Soviet Union and its ultimate collapse in 1989. Hell the only reason it lasted till then was from fear inducing dictators like Joseph Stalin forcing the masses to bow down at the point of a gun to the great comrade savior, communism.

From the late 19th century hippy we move on to the closet fagot of the early 20th century, John Maynard Keynes. JMK came up with the bright idea of putting a little communism in with capitalism (a government investment pool from taxes on the private sector). Well folks having a "little" communism is like having a "little" mental retardation. You ever seen anybody with a "little" mental retardation? I haven't, you're either blonde, I mean mentally retarded or not, no such thing as a "little" mental retardation. No folks a little communism is more like a cancer that eventually comes malignant.

Now I know I have not mentioned any queens. But do I need to? Let's just think about the word queen. Queen; a female ruler. Rulers are in charge of a countries finances, among other things. In other words a queen is a woman with an endless line of credit, can you think of anything more disastrous than that?

Why does this happen? Well I'm sounding like a scratched CD but everything must be paid for. Scarce resources must be allocated and it may not always seem fair and yes the bad guys sometimes win but an unhampered free market is the best means of distributing goods to consumers.

An unhampered market also allows mankind's greatest motive for improvement plenty of room to grow, greed. The desire for more has unlimited demand. Yes its true greed is the root of all evil, since evil consists of inventing more elaborate schemes of swindling. But it is also the root of all inventions that make our life more convenient, longer, and enjoyable. Some people reminisce about the

"Good Old Days", but as my mom would say, "The hell with the good old days, of no electric, getting water from a well in buckets, outhouses, cutting wood to heat an old drafty house, and barely scratching out a living".

But greed's greatest attribute is the limited supply of the desired outcome, wealth. Wealth is limited by the availability (or more appropriately the scarcity) of resources. Desirableness and availability go a long way in determining the price of an object. The balance or should I say imbalance of the two can be demonstrated by the following example. There are far more 1 ounce gold coins available than copies of this book but the price of gold is much higher than this book (much to my chagrin). That is why you have to look at Supply and Demand together to determine value. Some classical economists concentrated on supply i.e. J.B. Say coined the phrase; "Supply creates its own demand".

Then the Great Butcher of the unhampered market, Lord Keynes decided that the lack of demand creates depressions. For all his intelligence how the hell did he come up with this, since when do us humans desire less? I'll admit that there's merit in the old saying, "Having less is having more", but people just do not act in that manner, people simply want more.

Desires and needs create demand. Ability and availability create supply. But supply and demand cannot be separated in determining value.

The "New Economy, the New Economy", you would think the old familiar recession would end the talk about the "New Economy". The same ad manager that puts those soda pops in a different can with the word new on the can and the same horse piss in the can must have came up with the "New Economy" phrase. By the way Fucknut horse piss still tastes like horse piss. The economy is not new. There is still a market that requires buyers, sellers, products, and a medium of exchange. I'll be the first to admit that there are new products but that's one of the purposes of the market economy to bring new and better products. I hate to burst the bubble for these add wizards but bringing new products to market is and "old" economy concept. Besides if the economy is so "new" why are some of the biggest promoters of this campaign (politicians and policy makers) still pursuing the same old Bullshit policies?

Market basics:

- Buyers—have a need, at some point everyone is a buyer (consumer).
- Sellers—fulfill a need and on occasion through ingenuity they create a new desire by creating a new product.
- Products—what buyers demand and sellers provide.

- Medium of Exchange—just a way for buyers and sellers to come to terms on products. Remember its not the article that's used as a medium of exchange it's the amount of stuff you can get with it. Depending on the situation, location, timing and preferences this can vary.

- S & D—Dudleys of the world, markets must of course adhere to good ole supply and demand.

Now sure we could all live self sufficiently scratching out a bare bones living but Adam Smith proved in the "Wealth of Nations" that the division of labor makes us much wealthier and provides us an easier life by letting everyone perform smaller tasks on a regular basis and becoming more efficient at those tasks.

The bottom line is Supply and Demand. S&D works best through a free market system. Yes Mr. Market can be brutal and seem unfair, but for all you commies, bleeding heart liberals, and those wimps with no balls, well tough shit, its still the best system for allocating scarce resources. And as Ludwig von Mises stated, "Man has, there is no doubt, the power to destroy many things, and he has made in the course of history ample use of this faculty." And on many occasions has applied this faculty to damaging the free market. But no matter how many times man and his government philosophies try to eliminate Mr. Market, he reaches back and opens another can of wup ass. For no matter how hard these ignorant sons of bitches try to implement government controls of the market the simple law of supply and demand always overrules their best laid plans.

5

DON'T TRUST THE SO CALLED "EXPERTS"

October 21, 1929 Irving Fisher one of the most respected economists of the 20th Century offers this prognoses on the recent stock market declines, "Shaking out of the lunatic fringe that attempts to speculate on margin…prices of stocks during the boom had not caught up with their real value and would go higher." He believed this cause, "…the market had not yet reflected the beneficent effects of Prohibition, which made the American worker 'more productive and dependable".

October 25, 1929 Herbert Hoover following Black Thursday, "The fundamental business of the country…is on a sound and prosperous basis."

And following the expert opinions of these two prognosticators the American economy plunged head first into the Great Depression. All this leads me to the title of this chapter, "Don't trust the so called experts". Think of it this way, everyone in the United States has an opinion, but some are better at expressing their opinion than others. Well shit Dudley just because Joe Blow was blessed with the gift of gab doesn't mean he's right, just means he's full of hot air. And these experts have an agenda of their own, and guess what there are only 2 objectives for these people, one making money, two gaining more power. Of course they all claim to be helping you or the country. For example the stock brokers are not asking you to spend your money, its investing. The politicians (policy makers) are not going to raise your taxes, damn how long is America gonna fall for this line. By trusting these so called experts we put our trust in a limited number of individuals, which limits the opinions and direction of the nation. These limits give rise to opinions such as optimal rate of economic growth (*see figure 5-1*),

(FIG. 5-1)
KEYNES-RAMSEY RULE FOR DYNAMIC EFFICIENCY
(Optimal Economic Growth Bullshit Idea)

This formula states that the optimal amount of investment at any time t
(K') is equal to the distance-from-bliss divided by the marginal utility of
consumption:

$$K' = [B - U(C) + V(L)]/U' \text{ for all } t$$

K' = the optimal economic growth
B = level of Bliss (do you really think some mathematic formula can
measure this, these guys are warped)
U = Utility
C = Consumption
V(L) = disutility of Labor Supply

which within the framework of the current expert models makes sense. But why should the nation be limited to a model that constrains its possibilities. If we strip ourselves of these ideas, then there would be no limit to what the American people could accomplish. If we put more faith in our individual abilities, less trust and less money in the hands of these so called experts most of us would be better off. Of course some would be less fortunate, lets see, oh yeah those peckerheaded experts would be S.O.L. with less of our money to squander.

Now of course some people have an extraordinary talent and we can benefit from their talent. Yet finding these people with special abilities can be difficult and costly to find when it comes to investing. Most people do not put much time into finding the most talented advisors, much too often we put trust in the establishment, for example brokerage firms, just because of a title and the fact that Wall Street labels them as experts. But patience, diversification, and well defined goals of what you want can limit the dependence upon these 'experts', and diminish the need to find the most talented advisors. Keep in mind this fact; the experts have the same goals as you when finances and personal advancement is the topic and many times accomplishing their goals does not always correspond with accomplishing your goals.

For government policy makers the number one motive is expanding their programs, meaning a bigger share of our tax dollars. It doesn't matter if the program already adequately fulfills its purpose or in most cases is just a flat out waste of time and money; they just want to expand their influence. As for private sector experts their goal is simple; making more money. Sometimes this may directly conflict with your goals. A lot of these expert opinions contain stipulations; if this then that, if not this, if…if…if, if my aunt had balls she'd be my uncle.

Lets get a tad more specific on why these pricks are good for keeping balloons floating. I've broken the scheming bastards into two groups, government 'experts' (policy making apparatus), and private experts (consisting of analytical recommendations). By now you are fully aware of my distrust of anything linked to government dependence but when it comes to inept experts the government has an equal in the private sector, before all you non-libertarians (I mean commies) yell hooray one for our side, notice I said equal. Hell at least with the private sector 'experts' the rest of us have a choice whether to give them our money or not.

Financial analyst: make their living by you putting money into their products (recommendations). These analysts include mutual fund salesman, bank trust managers, insurance salesman, and stock brokers. And most of these people make their money from a commission not the performance of the products they sale. This can lead to a direct conflict with your personal needs. Notice the word analyst contains the word anal, and guess who's taking it in the rear? You guessed it, ole Dudley. Those pricks make their money whether you do or not.

Lets move onto the major leagues of Financial Analysis, the big brokerage firms on Wall Street. These hot-shots make overall portfolio recommendations (money allocation, i.e. 70% stocks 30% bonds) and recommendations on individual financial assets (stocks, bonds, ect). There are several different (supposedly different) brokerage firms, but it seems all their analysts are from the same Dudley Dumbshit family. Many of these tend to make the same recommendations. And if you think about it logically there is one very good reason for them to follow the herd as an analyst, survival. If one analyst decides to buck the trend with a recommendation and is wrong, he's going to be fired. But if he follows the herd and winds up in the same pile of herd turds as the others, he just smells like the rest and keeps his job.

Speaking of the recommendations of these Wall Street gurus here's a list of some terminology they use on stock recommendations:

Buy
Moderate buy
Hold
Moderate sell
Sell
Accumulate
Acquire
Liquidate
Strong buy
Strong sell
Moderate hold
Obtain
Purchase
Sector perform
Market perform
Underperform
Out perform
Neutral
Trading buy

Recommended list

Underweight

Equal weight

Overweight

LT buy (I reckon that means light buy then again maybe its ass backwards and means buy little turds)

Add (their upgrade from this was buy, I ain't shitting you, I wish I was making this stuff up but I'm not that creative, apparently the folks at Credit Lyonnais Sec. think you can add a stock without buying it.)

Significant outperform

Ahhhh shit now, am I picking stocks or a harem, goddamn just tell me buy, hold or sell, don't give me a fucking dictionary. Hell are these pricks analyst or long winded lawyers. And this list is buy no means exhaustive, I just got lazy and decided to quit writing the crap down.

Working right along with the brilliance of the analysts are the stockbrokers. These guys make money for themselves and their firm by executing trades. Now remember these bastards are like a whore, they don't care about the quality of the transaction just that there is a transaction. The more you trade the more money they make, no matter what the stock does after your purchase. Related to brokers are mutual fund salesman; equivalent of a used car salesman, they no little about the products their selling and far less about what you really need and want, but they do come with a long line of bullshit. Branching out further on this family tree come the insurance salesman, no need to expand upon their competence or lack thereof, the name speaks volumes: insurance salesman.

Economist, why are people awed by this title, thinking that these individuals posses great knowledge of the future in the world markets. Go to a college campus and visit the econ department, most wound up their because they bombed out of engineering, mathematics, chemistry or some other real discipline, (word of advice don't actually start a conversation with these people unless you feel a great desire to be bored beyond your senses). Most economists make an attempt at economic forecasts, these forecasts try to predict future human action based on numbers gathered from past events. Hell us humans can't predict tomorrows weather with complex equipment let alone next years results on the DOW.

With the allusion to past numbers in the previous paragraph that brings to mind another band of lame duck professionals, statisticians. If you have something to argue and need something to back your argument, I suggest you go see these people. Believe me, they can come up with the numbers you need to prove your point, their livelihood depends on it. But once they come up with their numbers don't ask them to take into consideration any obvious human factors that may disqualify a particular case, for the numbers must have taken that into consideration. Hell yeah, if a 23 year old male is 6'3" 225lbs and bench presses 300 plus, he can hit a baseball 500 feet, doesn't matter that he's blind, he can still hit it 500 feet,

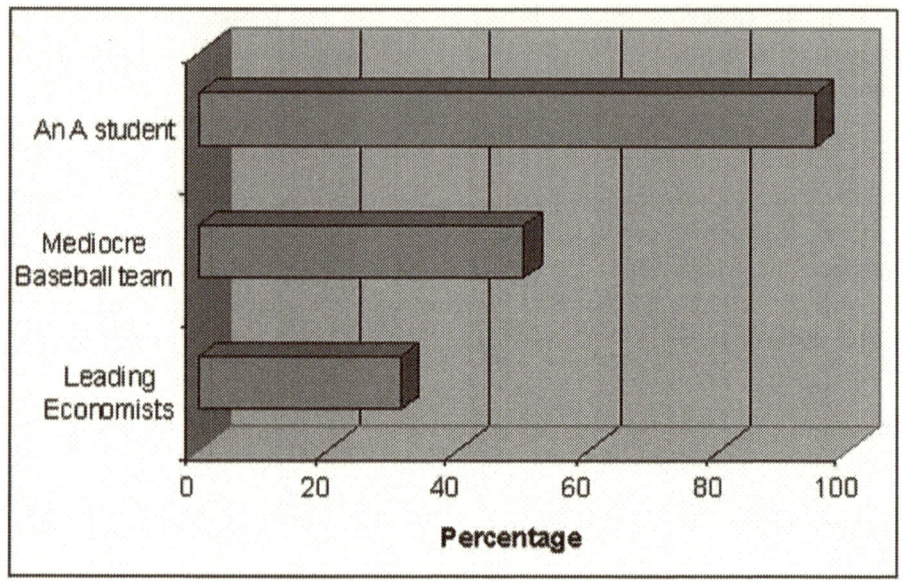

(FIG 5-2) Comparison of Interest Rate Predictions of
Leading Economists in Wall Street Journal
1982-2002

And this was for predictions of just 6 months out, 31% accuracy. Good thing they don't hunt for a living with that kind of accuracy.

hint if you own a baseball team don't let a statistician make the final judgment on a future prospect.

Oh by the way let me point out that the numbers and analysis put out by statisticians and economists are considered essential to decisions made by government policy makers. Yep your tax rates, interest rates, margin rates and bank reserves are determined by policy makers based on the work of the aforementioned individuals, (hope your able to sleep tonight). If you listen to the politicians and bureaucrats (congratulations to those who don't) they can tell you things are great when your in the unemployment line, while at the same time telling you what it takes to get us out of a recession, how to slow down an overheating economy; by the way "overheating" economy means things are too good and slowing down is needed and slowing the economy is one thing policy makers can do with devastating effect. Excuse me I have a question. If these Nostradamuses (Nostradumbasses) are so good at predicting what will happen and fixing and/or preventing the bad things, why do we still have recessions?

How about I criticize a couple of specific expert opinions by these stellar individuals, specifically economists (just some pet peeves of mine). First is the Optimal Savings Rate Theory. What a big ole pile of horse dung this one is. How the hell can these Dudley's claim to know the optimal savings rate. This is exceptional hot air when they claim a society can save too much. Their argument is that an advanced society has no room for technological advancement therefore less need to save for research and development and needs to spend more to keep the economy going. BULLLLLLL...SHITTTT, there is always the possibility of a revolutionary invention that changes the way people live even in an advanced society, for example trains, cars, planes, and computers. If anything an advanced society could save more and make even greater accomplishments, possibly space travel, finding a better source of energy, hell the possibilities are endless. Economists speak of hoarding money as a societal evil, all it means is that producers are not bringing the right products to market in order to compel consumers to part with their money, it ain't got jack shit to do with an optimal savings rate.

But my biggest gripe is against the long held belief that the economy must grow at a certain rate, (for the U.S. this is believed to be between 3-5%). That's arbitrary if not out right wrong at best. How the fuck do those knuckleheads in DC know how fast the economy is capable of growing (shit they can't even balance their checkbook and come up with the current budget). The basic argument behind the growth rate theory is that if the economy grows to "fast" say at 10%, (the measure generally used for economic growth is GDP), that businesses, government and consumers will outstrip available resources causing disastrous inflation. Now think about the logic in this concept, the economy is getting bigger creating more stuff for you and I and this is considered a bad thing? Now the common policy to rid us of this disastrous evil is to raise interest rates. Interest rates are just the price of money. Yeah to prevent the devastation of inflation (higher prices) they raise the price of money. In an advanced society that is the one commodity that purchases all other goods so they raise its price. Doesn't that theoretically raise the price of every thing else? Another possibility is to raise taxes so you have less to spend, of course they turn around and use that money to buy a fleet of nuclear subs, side note: revenues from tax increase = $1 billion, outlays for fleet of subs = $2 billion. Now without these interventions if the economy really did "overheat" the price of stuff (cars, food, movies) would go up of its own accord naturally. Why arbitrarily create inflation to slow the economy based on an event that may not happen and if it does will provide the needed cure on its own with absolutely no interference from the stinking feds. Besides why can't the economy grow at 10 percent? We do not know that it can't, and thanks to the current economic system we will never find out. As in the Optimal savings rate example, policy makers can't account for technological break throughs. It seems to me a higher growth rate might spur better products due to the tougher competition to keep ahead of the game. I equate this to a professional baseball player who advances through each level, starting from the Little League to the Majors. At each level he must become accustomed to hitting faster and better pitching on a regular basis at each advancement, and different players advance at different rates, some reach the Majors at 20, some their late twenties.

By setting these extremely arbitrary policies society handicaps its economic potential. These policies remove the potential of all consumers to vote with their dollars on a daily basis in the market to decide the best direction of the market, Adam Smith called this the invisible hand of the market. Instead interventionist policies entrust the direction of economic activity into the hands of a few. This sets society back by quelling ingenuity, through control of beliefs and preventing innovation. In the long run it can lead to disaster by making economic shocks worse. Let private individuals collectively take control of human destiny not these so called experts.

Lets see, experts, can not predict the future, have trouble interpreting the present, hell they can hardly tell you what happened in the past. Even if by some miracle one of these experts could give a good idea of what the future holds, you're trying to find this guru out of the countless fools that fell out of the Dudley Dumbshit family tree. Then to add insult to injury if you did secure this sages information it may or may not help you. Although intrusting to your own judgment and allowing others to act upon their own judgment may not guarantee things work out as planned, at least the opportunity of it working out the way you wanted exists, the alternative guarantees it will not.

6

PERSONAL INVESTMENT

"Investment is most intelligent when it is most business like." (Benjamin Graham)

Remember the key to investing is like any business, making good deals. If you treat investment purchases like going to the grocery store (look for bargains), in the long run you will be much more successful.

Now if your one of those Peckerheads that burns a hole in his pocket every time you get some money, well skip this chapter, if you can't save you can't invest. Hell if your in the spendthrift category why are you reading this at all. Oh yeah, Dudley Dumbshit personified done blew all his money and can't afford anything but dollar books from B. Walton's bookstore. And this brings me to the answer of the most asked financial question, "What's the best way to increase my investments?" And I always give the same answer, cut your expenses, of course no one wants to hear that, but it does work.

Investment planning basics begin with the budget, that addresses needs, allocation, diversification, and followed up with a backup plan. Yes a backup plan, cause Shit Happens. As with any plan discipline is needed to succeed, but you have to allow for some flexibility (If your getting your ass kicked 21-0 at the half you need to adjust). The backup plan allows for adjustment but the budget is were the most discipline is required.

Budget, AAAAAAHHHHH!!!!! Holy shit, Armageddon, Apocalypse Now, WWIII, hell the way people cringe at the word you'd think it meant the end of time. Remember those old cereal commercials try it Mike, he likes, he likes it! People always complain about being broke, well complaining ain't gonna fix it. And if Dudley Dumbshit plans on fixing it he needs a budget.

There a differing methods of figuring a budget and this list is by no means exhaustive, but it's a start; down to the last cent (anal method), pay day hey day (my personal method), mattress method, left over method, direct deposit (DD), and of course the ever popular fuck it method (the non budget). And within each budget you must prioritize, yeah, choices, choices, too many choices so little time and not enough money.

The last cent (anal) method will most likely save you the most money, but it requires the most discipline, and can be a royal pain in the ass. This requires coordinating your fiscal plans with your schedule (since it requires keeping an extremely close eye on your expenditures). Planning your time for time is money. Planning out expenditures in money and time has to be prioritized, starting with the essentials. And when I say essentials I am not talking about shopping at Macy's, I mean food (shit even Dudley has to eat), the mortgage (got to have a place to roost), and of course beer (gotta get through the day somehow). Once the essentials are taking care of one can work toward their financial goals (provided Dudley set some goals). Reaching ones financial goals really doesn't require great intelligence or luck (although they greatly facilitate the effort), but it does require discipline and patience. If the anal method is your choice of attack after priorities are set, one must schedule out events (bills, pay day, investments and fun). Supreme anal users keep receipts and put revenue and expenditures into a spreadsheet to get an exact idea of were the money is going on a monthly basis. And of course this requires a record keeping system for filing your paper trail. Yes the anal method received its name for a good reason, it's a huge fucking pain in the ass.

A good adaptation of the anal method is the surprisingly painless Dudley Dumbshit special the D.D. (Direct Deposit) method. It only requires applying the anal method for a short period of time, say 3 months. After the 90 day sentence is served you should have a good idea of what your spending and what could be saved. Then setup direct deposits and/or allotments to investment accounts, and possible direct payments for bills, and live it up on whatever is left. This works great for those with less than perfect disciplined spending habits, for if you ain't got it you don't miss it, or spend it in this case. The hardest part about this concept is just getting started. The filling out of the legal ease type documents and filling in the mile long bank routing number, and account numbers, (I didn't mention Uncle Slam Ya, but I'm sure he's in there with some token paperwork and a hand in your pocket). But once through the paper annoyance trail, this becomes a very effective investment tool.

For those with a little more discipline (or those who fear the electronic transfers), the pay day and have a hey day method may work. Just plan on sitting down with your checkbook on pay day and paying off the bills due for that pay period, sending off pre-determined amounts for investments, then just blow the rest. This allows a tad more flexibility than the DD method in that if you get an extra windfall of cash in a pay period you can just pencil in a bit more on the checks going toward investments, or it will allow you to take care of unforeseen emergencies without the hassle of digging into investment accounts or taking out high interest rate short term loans (emergencies should be accounted for in all methods but there is the fudge factor and that factor is human error). I personally prefer this over the DD system for its easier to adjust when you have changes in your pay. For instance when you get a raise your less likely to change your allotment amount due to the aforementioned paperwork. But if your in the habit of sitting down on pay day and writing out checks it only requires a simple change of the amount you put on the check.

One could change the Pay Day method around to sending out all your investments the day before pay day, using whatever amount you have left over. This requires a more disciplined spending habit, for its difficult not to buy that new video game if you actually have the cash available for it. But if your one of those whose addicted to saving (Yeah right) then this can be very effective, for if this is the case it may create a situation were you try to exceed your savings goals. This could also be adapted in different ways, the mattress method, stuff the money away for an extended period of time say a year and dump it into some investments.

And for those who just don't give a big rats ass, or have faith in the Social Security System (SUCKER) there's the ever popular Fuck It method. Make it spend it, spend some more and to hell with tomorrow, live for today. Now for those who plan on working till they die and realize Social Security is a joke, my hats of to you, the fuck it method will work just fine. I envy those who can live that way with little or no worries for the future. For those of you who plan on working to Gabriel blows his horn, I still suggest setting aside some for a rainy day, (6 months wages is a general rule of thumb). For the suckers who are counting on Social Insecurity, well you have got to be the poster child for the entire Dudley Dumbshit community, putting your faith in something that takes your money to pay you back later and doesn't even give you the full amount back let alone an interest that keeps up with inflation. If you want to depend on the communist manifesto and its Social Insecurity payments, well don't expect any sympathy from me, FUCK IT.

Now if you plan on working towards a more traditional retirement with a pension near the age of sixty-five, keep a few things in mind. Set priorities, without this you can't give direction to your budget plan. Without the plan you can't allocate scarce resources. And if you don't allocate resources appropriately, I guarantee a couple of things that won't be scarce are the amount of hours you have to work and the number of creditors banging at your door. And by the way if Dudley is too busy working the stud next door is going to be doing some banging of his own with your lonely little wife.

Once you have brain washed yourself into a saving program the next most important item after the actual saving is what to do with your money, and the key here is diversification. Yes all them stories about not putting all your eggs in one basket apply to all of us in the Dumbshit family. But if you know a sure fire 100% guaranteed way to earn an outlandish return, for example growing pot (of course you may windup in an 8X8 cell with Bubba and his 10" rectum reamer) by all means pass on deworsification. But for the rest of us who don't know of a full proof investment and want to practice Bubba avoidance, diversification is key. And diversification begins with asset allocation.

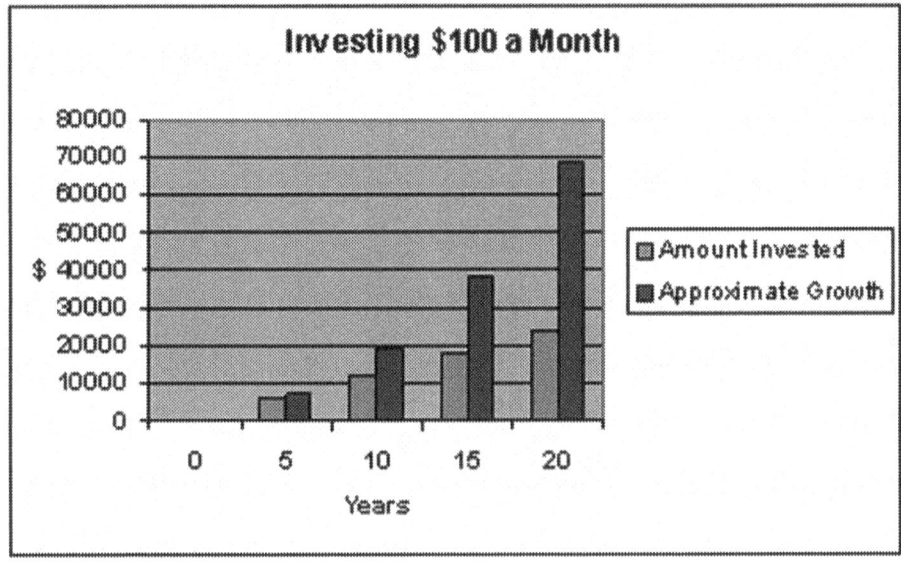

(FIG 6-1)

This chart gives the approximate value of investing 100 dollars a month for twenty years in a stock market fund. This uses a 10% growth, which historically is low for the stock market, its generally been 11 percent, but I felt a tad pessimistic when I made this graph. Your contribution for the period would be $24,000 growing to approximately $70,000 and this is erring on the side of caution.

There are several factors to consider when thinking of asset allocation that come before choosing investment categories let alone specific investments within each category. One has to account for their age, time (investment horizon), likes and dislikes, and a realistic evaluation of ones personality (mind set) which will determine your risk tolerance.

Of the asset allocation factors age is the most important. Face the facts you are not going to live forever, so each investment must be evaluated for its risk and return, pros and cons based on age. Unfortunately we all know that we will die we just don't know when, Ahh shit man lives in desperation and dies in despair, and women guarantee it. Age determines needs. If you're a young college grad, the possibility of a future prison term (marriage), must be considered, then knockin up the little woman, housing needs, and of course the very expensive purchase of ending your prison term (divorce). As you get older the needs change and if the cards were played correctly, Dudley may be able to retire, and must live off of those savings, but now has grandchildren to spoil, more medical bills and Depends.

Getting more specific age is heavily weighted in determining the importance of different types of financial assets. The young should be heavily weighted toward stocks, old fucks should be geared toward fixed income securities.

Time (investment horizon) is also important, meaning how long from now do you need the money from a given investment. I know, sounds the same as the age factor. But I separate it since it can be different. For example your driving a 5 year old Taurus with 90,000 miles on it and figure you need another car in 3 years. Well you could be 25 or 55 at this point. Since your investment horizon is less than 5 years you should probably stay clear of stocks even if you're the 25 year old. Or maybe you want to put a new born through college in 18 years, could be your baby or your grandbaby, but its still 18 years away, meaning you should be looking at stocks initially, and possibly having the money shifted to a more stable investment as college grows closer for the recipient. Naturally the shorter the investment horizon the more conservative the investment should be, although in reality people tend to be more aggressive in that situation, thinking oh no I need to double my money in 3 years so they take more chances. Well Dudley, I got some bad news, if you need to double your money in 3 years you better get a second job. Remember time and the tide wait for nobody plan ahead and apply a suitable time frame for each investment goal.

Mr. Dumbshit pulls in from work turns on the news, hears the Dow dropped 300 points, promptly browns his tailor made britches, calls his wife a bitch for listening to that financial advisor, gets 2 hours sleep, drags ass out of sack next morning, shows up late for work, the peckerheaded boss tells you the Dow is now heading for another triple digit loss, you sock him in the nose and now your standing in the unemployment line. If your one of those who loses sleep every time the market drops you probably should not be heavily invested in stocks, no matter what your age. Yes over the long haul the neighbor with ice water in his veins that's fully invested in stocks will probably have more at retirement than you, but if you die of a heart attack at 45 cause you can't stand the stress of the market that extra return just ain't worth it. This is very important, a realistic judgment of ones risk tolerance will allow many sweet dreams, while an unrealistic assessment will cause nightmares.

Also keep in mind when dividing up your investment dollars your personal likes, dislikes and abilities. If you do something you enjoy you will probably be good at it (or at least not mind being bad) and if you can make money to boot, well Dudley that's a big fat bonus. For example if you like collecting coins, you might consider putting a little extra cash towards that endeavor as an investment. Be careful not to get carried away especially if you have a little success and think you have found the midas touch, then bet the house, for your liable to wind up under a bridge with Willie the Wino. Having expertise in certain areas may also give you an advantage in some investment areas. If you're a corn farmer get involved in commodity futures. Take advantage of your talents, look for investments that allow you to use what you already know. But if your like yours truly and studied econ in college, well sorry your shit out of luck.

Once you've decided how much to allocate to each asset category (stocks, real estate, bonds, ect) you have to diversify within each asset category. For example, the money you allocate toward stocks should not be all in one stock or even in just one mutual fund, or if involved in real estate try to avoid relying on one piece of rental property to heavily. Diversifying in real estate can be difficult do to the costs, if you are involved with just one piece of real estate such as a rental property try to avoid making it your only source of income. Allocation in stocks should involve more than one account. Open an IRA, a brokerage account, get involved in a 401K, open a mutual fund and make sure that the accounts are not the same type. Don't have a S&P 500 tracking fund as the only investment in all the accounts. Within a fixed income portion diversify among bonds (corporate, junk, AAA, government), savings account, and money market accounts.

If your world goes to hell in a hand basket or you don't quite meet your investment goals it helps to have a backup plan. If you can't afford that hundred acre estate with a mansion, maybe one acre with a log cabin will suffice (look at the bright side less to mow), or maybe that Porsche is a tad too much, get a Miata (better on gas anyway).

Investing requires funds (it takes money to make money). To get the required funds takes discipline, a plan, referred to here as the budget. After the budget has produced the required funds allocation with diversification is needed to protect and enhance the funds allowing one to meet goals sought. Having a backup plan gives a little more security or in better terminology an escape rout, for plans do fail.

7

POLITICS (LOVE YOUR COUNTRY BUT FEAR YOUR GOVERNMENT)

"It is the highest impertinence and presumption,…in kings and ministers, to pretend to watch over the economy of private people, and restrain their expense, either by sumptuary laws, or by prohibiting importation of foreign luxuries. They are themselves the greatest spendthrifts in the society… If their own extravagance does not ruin the state that of their subjects never will." Adam Smith

In laymen's terms Mr. Smith means its those pricks in Washington City that will brake this country not the average Joe down at the mill. Our deficit is measured in trillions (yes that's plural) of dollars, TRILLIONS (and no that ain't no typo as is *tr* or *b* or *m*). You say so what it doesn't belong to me, wrong Dudley, thanks to that mountain of debt your guaranteed to pay 18 cents on the dollar in taxes just for interest. That's 18 tax dollars out of a hundred that buys you Jack Shit. This year the financially irresponsible pukes in Washington will spend about $230 billion on interest, only two other government programs will spend more, defense and Social Security. Think about it Dudley that interest has to be paid, no matter which lying fucking party controls Congress, no matter what Dumbass we put in the White House, that has to be paid, then those pricks start dipping in your pocket for even more. And when they dip into our pockets, they say it will only increase your taxes by a small amount, in some cases less than 1%, well shit that ain't much. But God Damn, lets add up all those "little taxes", FICA tax, property tax, registrations, sales tax, sin tax, and a host of others, well I'll be it adds up to about half your check! Then some leftist liberal says, "At least we're still free". Horseshit Dudley, a mans freedom can be measured by the amount of taxes he must pay, and by god this half ass freedom ain't going to cut it. Wake Up People!! Being free is not easy and it begins with us citizens taking on some responsibility, and we can gain that responsibility at the voting booth. Put someone in who will finally dismantle the current system, end our one way street towards Socialism, start using warfare for defense and not as a foreign policy tool, and someone who will take on some financial responsibility.

"Shortly after election, Jefferson, in a letter titled 'Reconciliation and Reform,' wrote this. 'The steady character of our countrymen is a rock to which we may safely moor; unequivocal in principle, reasonable in manner. We should be able to hope to do a great deal of good to the cause of freedom and harmony.' I will be guided by President's Jefferson's sense of purpose, to stand for principle, to be reasonable in manner, and above all, to do great good for the cause of freedom and harmony." Weasel headed lying Dubya shortly after being declared President.

"Much time has passed since Jefferson arrived for his inauguration. The years and changes accumulate. But the themes of this day he would know: our nation's grand story of courage, and its simple dream of dignity." Dubya at inauguration

"We've been there for 90 days since the cessation of major operations, I never have expected Thomas Jefferson to emerge in Iraq in a 90-day period."

Give me a brake while I puke my guts out! President George W. Bush quoting Thomas Jefferson and saying he believes in the ideas of our founding fathers. Obviously he has never read the actual content of Mr. Jefferson's writings on government, hell he can't even read his own middle initial. One of the most ardent fears of our founding fathers was the fear of big government, yet Dubya increased government expenditures to the largest amount in the nations history, and increased the powers of the government to levels our ancestors would have revolted over (and did revolt over), all in the name of national security in the wake of the terrorist attacks. And how long did it take to catch Old Son of Bitch Bin Lying?

"Freedom and liberty always refer to interhuman relations. A man is free as far as he can live and get on without being at the mercy of arbitrary decisions on the part of other people." Ludwig von Mises

Politicians toss the words of liberty and freedom around without explaining what their meaning of those words are. True freedom (liberty) is the ability of the individual to act without interference on ones beliefs provided those actions do not trample on others. This includes freedom of thought, expression and most definitely economic freedom. Freedom and liberty are derived from human cooperation. Society creates freedom by mutual protection of individuals. These were the beliefs of our founding fathers when they created this nation, but the words of those great men when used by our leaders today are nothing more than decoration. The notions of true freedom and liberty today are an ideal not a reality. The worst part about this destruction of classical liberalism is that we the American people do nothing as if we are brain washed or don't care. I have already heavily criticized those that govern, and they justly deserve it. But the reality is that we the citizens have allowed this to happen. It is a shame that so many men and women have died trying to make the dream of liberty a reality, yet we keep drifting in the opposite direction despite their sacrifices. Today thousands put their lives on the line each day for the ideal that in reality is not practiced. Free societies with individual liberty are not easy; it requires hard work, study, participation, and compassion for our fellow man. The latter, compassion, has been turned over to the care of the government, and with its tendency towards bureaucratic red tape compassion and feeling are lost, its an absolute mistake. People with hardships or just plain laziness start expecting handouts from the government. Many people believe that the government should take care of the less fortunate for they feel people are to cruel to help their fellow man. How many times have you heard someone say, "I'm not helping that's what taxes are for". This may be why some people seem cruel, but hell when half your check goes to the tax collector and you see welfare recipients doing spot and steal work, spotting of the day and stealing of the night, naturally you will feel that way.

Not only have we sat back and allowed our economic freedom to be trampled on, even yet more horrifying we have allowed our personal liberty's whittled away, all for a safer society according to advocates of these unconstitutional laws. Obviously these people have never heard the Ben Franklin quote, "They that can give up essential liberty to obtain temporary safety deserve neither liberty nor safety." To make matters worse when these laws are written for our "safety" the policy makers always say there not intended for the average citizen, just a special group or in some cases non U.S. citizens. For example the terrorism bills past to defend us are not intended for use in anything but terrorist acts like that on the Word Trade Center. People really are subject to brainwashing, either that or their just plain stupid. The ink had not even dried on those terrorists bills (i.e. the Unpatriot Act), when government prosecutors were using them on crimes committed by Americans who had no links to terrorists networks such as Al Queida, Asscroft liberty steeling act has been used to convict smalltime hillbilly pot growers and inter city pimps, not exactly life threatening terrorist groups. The DC sniper shootings, for example, prosecutors talked of using this new law. Granted what those 2 assholes did was terrorifying, but they were not members of a terrorist organization, 2 cold blooded killers yes acting on their own warped fantasies, but not terrorists, and no new terrorist bill is needed to convict murderers.

Another liberty stealing law is the Bank Secrecy Act, but don't think for a minute the word secrecy is referring to your protection. What it refers to is when your bank processes a large transaction for you (or any transaction that seems "suspicious"), they must report this secretly and without your consent to the U.S. Attorney's office. *www.privacilla.org/government/banksecrecyact.html* Talk about a Gestapo law, they take your money with little or no explanation other than some government official believes no one needs to travel with that much money unless its for illegal activity, so therefore this law can't hurt the average citizen. This law is just inherently flawed, how the hell do they know my business doesn't require my needing $10,000. Worse yet is this law is intended for use against fighting a nonviolent crime (drug smuggling), a crime in which no ones personal rights was trampled on. The real criminals here are the SOB's who wrote the law!

Pre-emptive striking, global militarism, the CIA, and Homeland Security, yet more calls for our money in the guise of "safety". These ideas supposedly defend us from eminent attacks within our borders and from abroad, yet people like Sadam Hussien still come to power and 911 becomes known as something other than an emergency phone number. Oh but what about WWII, if we would have entered it earlier "Pre-emptive strike", less Americans would have died, and anybody who thinks different is sticking their head in the sand and being shortsighted. This is always the rallying cry for war against people like Sadam, remember Hitler. What? Entering a conflict that 2 or more other nations are already involved in earlier saves lives for an idle country? Lets see, if we had entered WWII earlier, Germany would have had more men, due to the natural attrition of war, and depending how much earlier we entered we might have had to take on them and the Russians, since they were in a nonaggresion pack with the Krauts, and being Commies they hated our guts anyway. But Hitler didn't like the Russians, that's why he attacked them, but if we would have joined up earlier with the Limies in the west do you really think Adolf would have taken on another "Mein Kamf" in the east just for good measure? I doubt it, hell the Russians might just have entered as one of the Axis Powers and then we would have had to fight both of them at their full strength, sounds like a real fucking bonehead idea to me. I would argue we entered the war in Europe to soon or possibly we should not have at all. Oh but the Nazis would have moved on us after defeating the British. 1. So fucking what, which war maneuver in general causes more casualties; defensive or offensive? Lets see if they come after us we would have been entrenched and at full strength, by going the invasion route their entrenched, ever read about D-Day and the shores of Normandy, we won but damn what a price to pay. Another example of this concept is Robert E. Lee during our Civil War. Lee demonstrated great ability to defend Richmond with a much smaller force than those opposed to him, but the tide of that war changed when he went on the offensive at Gettysburg, and this is an example of an invasion on the same continent, not across the Atlantic. Hell the god damn Russians stopped Hitler and they didn't even have enough guns for all their troops. Oh but Germany was much more technologically advanced and so determined to take over the world that they would have if we had not entered the war. Does anyone remember the Battle of Britain? Apparently not, well here is a little refresher. The Battle of Britain was an air assault of the German Luftwaffe to soften the defenses of Britain for a land invasion across the English Channel. And if my knowledge of history is correct the limies won, a little ole island no bigger than the state of Georgia, wupped the big bad Nazis of Germany. Well let me see how much help did the British have? NONE, the Frogs had already performed their national pastime and surrendered. And this all took place between July 10 and October 31, *1940!* Yes, 31 October 1940, a full 13 months before Pearl Harbor. Now you still expect me to believe the United States was threatened by a German invasion? How the hell were they going to attack us all the way across the Atlantic, when they were stopped at the English Channel? They never, never even attempted a land invasion of England, unless you count the Germanic invasions of the 5th and 6th centuries. Hell the last successful land invasion of Britain was by William the Conqueror with his victory at the Battle of Hastings in 1066, and that S.O.B. had been promised the English crown at the age of 8, and why? He had Limy blood in him, Royal blood at that! Did I mention that the Battle of Britain took place between July 1940 and October 1940, oh yes I believe I did. Lets see, the bull headed Russians weren't dragged into the war till June 21, 1941. Yet with all the evidence presented to me that the Brits held the Germans off with absolutely no help, I'm still supposed to believe we Americans needed to enter the war sooner to save American lives. The only reason people are convinced that we Americans were the key factor in winning the war for the Allies is that the winners write the history books. Since we came out of WWII in better shape than anyone else; Europe was devastated, along with parts of Asia, that made us the winners. National pride and political arrogance also fostered the idea of us as having saved the world from the evils of Nazism.

"Ask not what your country can do for you, but what you can do for your country." John F. Kennedy

Quit expecting the government too solve our problems. Its been proven time and time again that government fixes are part of the problem. Politicians have done one thing well and that's convincing us that if this or that program is passed they can fix the problem. Yet they never do, and do they admit their mistake, no they only say the program is under funded, we need more taxes, and recycle the same old worthless ideas. But Dudley Dumbshit USA keeps falling for the BS these politicians put out and worse yet most apparently believe that the government can fix their problems. Though I don't see how the hell people think someone sitting in DC knows what's better for those out in Butfuck Idaho, hell how does the state capitol or even the county know what's best for you. Shit, how many of you would trust your next door neighbors to make an important decision for you? No, the words Kennedy spoke are not easy to live by, but there damn sure worth living for. At least we are not subject to the arbitrary decision of the government and thereby able to depend on our own abilities and beliefs without interference from others. If these people like the government controlling their lives, well Dudley, the line at your local military recruiters isn't exactly crowded, so march your happy ass over there and sign up! They'll be more than glad to accommodate you with even more than all the government interference and control of your life than you can imagine.

The President just took a week long vacation to Camp David, or Congress went on summer recess, and people complain. No need to complain when their on vacation, that's time for celebration, hell they're not altogether conjuring up new schemes to screw us over. "No one's life, liberty, or property are safe while the legislature is in session." *Part of Murphy's Law.* Politics should not be a full-time job, make them live by the laws they create. I remember visiting the state capitol for the Commonwealth of Virginia and during the tour the guide mentioned that the state legislators only meet for a 30-45 day session. A couple from New Jersey was just amazed that the session was so short. Hell I live in Virginia, apparently that's too damn long. The legislators of Virginia must have spent to long thinking about that word "Commonwealth", and decided the residents money should be pooled into a common treasury, for they ain't met a tax they didn't like. Its just down right amazing that people expect the government to do so much, when all that does is limit their own ability to do what they want. The ones it hurts the most are the ones who want it to do the most. If those leftist liberal college campus hippies advocated limited government with true liberty they would have many more opportunities to express and follow through on their tree-hugging beliefs. They seem to hate what they call corporate exploitation of the consumer. The poor consumer, hell if people don't like a company I hope they got sense enough not to buy their products. In a free market system you have the choice not to buy as much as you have a choice to buy. With a government intervention, you have no choice, you pay the tax whether you support the program or not.

"It's the Economy Stupid." Bill Clinton

Well if it is the economy, why don't we put an economist in the White House instead of a crooked ass lawyer? It is truly amazing the way people vote, actually its fucking STUPID! D.D.S.A.'s (Dudley DumbShits of America) vote to take power out of their own hands and give it to an ever expanding and intrusive bunch of government bureaucrats and agents. Maybe I'm wrong and the Dudley's are exercising their freedom by voting in more power to the politicians on purpose. Just maybe the voters are blessed with enough intelligence to realize just how incompetent they are and feel that the central authorities are gods chosen with all the brilliance to make better decisions for the whole country, nah the voters are just stupid. Our ever brilliant leaders often mention the "American Heritage" handed down by the likes of Washington and Jefferson. Maybe these dumbasses should do a little less talking about the founding fathers and a lot more reading. The "American Heritage" and ideals they speak of did not envision the worlds largest bureaucracy, invasion of nations that posed no military threat to our borders, loss of personal liberties, a 50% tax rate, and an unarmed citizenry. Did I tell you all how much I hate it when those Capitol Hill Con Artists quote our Revolutionary Hero's, well its worth mentioning again. Speaking of our Revolutionary Hero's, that was damn noble of our lawbreakers (oops I mean lawmakers), to honor our greatest hero with his own day, oh shit excuse me ole George has to split that day with likes of all that followed him including Nixon and Slick Willy, Presidents Day. Holy Shit even Columbus got his own day and for what he got lost! Lets not forget the Great Emancipator, MLK gets his own day for making a march and a speech, but the man who freed all the slaves has to split that Presidents day thing (Ironically with several men who owned slaves).

How brilliant does this concept sound, increasing your expenditures when your income is decreasing (excessive debt)? Or how many Redneck wives would approve of their loving husbands dropping a V8 in that 6 cylinder mustang the day after he got fired? And how many husbands would agree to by a new washing machine in that situation? Oh Shit no Dudley, sounds like piss poor financial advise. Then why in Sam Hell do we think this is just hunky dory for Uncle Sam? For example in February 2003 the stock market is about 40% off its highs, unemployment is rising, the economy sucks and George Dubya Bush wants to attack SooDamn Insane over in Iraq, who's military isn't capable of whipping a pack of Cub Scouts. Now even if you consider Sadam a horrible person, the fact is people in this country are scared and worried about the economy. You have to way your priorities, and as President of this country Dubya's priorities are to the citizens of the U.S. not those in Iraq. Asking the American tax payer to fund a $75 billion war when they are worried about their jobs is just ludicrous.

People are selfish and uncharitable, therefore government needs to help the less fortunate? What? People trust those crooked politicians to be more charitable than themselves? Hell all that does is guarantee money is filtered to those people and groups that helped the given politician get elected. But some goes to help the children. Yeah giving money to jobless moms is just great, hell they may even decide to breed again so the rest of us can pay for the creation of some more welfare trash. Damn good idea you bleeding heart, tree hugging liberal. Don't those dumbasses realize that for every dollar Uncle takes, that's one less dollar for them to give to the cause they believe is the most needy. Also, the inefficiencies of government means that a small percentage of the government "charity" dollars actually go to the people they intend to help.

Taxes, taxes, and more taxes; people bitch and complain about taxes but keep on putting the same donkeys and elephants in office. But Dudley says; I have no choice, I voted for the lesser of two evils. Bullshit, there are other parties, (even though the Pink Elephants and Jackasses have done a good job of convincing other wise), hint the Libertarian Party. But of course if you benefit from the current system, well, you lazy piece of welfare trash!

"Still one thing more, fellow citizens, a wise and frugal government, which shall restrain men from injuring one another, which shall leave them otherwise free to regulate their own pursuits of industry and improvement, and shall not take from the mouth of labor the bread it has earned. This is the sum of good government..." Thomas Jefferson's 1st Inaugural address, March 4, 1801.

Two hundred years later and lets do the addition for Mr. Jefferson's formula, well, once all the subtracting is down they ain't much left to add. A $6 trillion national debt (that's not frugal), first strike military operations that create more terrorist threats (that's not wise), and laws that incarcerate people for victimless crimes (that's not allowing men to pursuit their own interest). Plus (actually another minus), all the above diverts funds away from the governments ultimate purpose, restraining people from injuring others, for an example take a walk through Baltimore at about 2 in the morning.

The current tax system, talk about taking from the mouth of labor. The current system is also extremely intrusive and does not allow individuals to fully pursuit their own self interests. Not only does the current system penalize hard work with transfers of income; it tells you what to do with portions it supposedly allocates to you. What do I mean by this, Social Security and Medicare Insurance. Social Security doesn't even allow you to decide what type of investment to put the money in, and Medicare forces you into a shitty healthcare plan with very few choices. What if your married to a doctor, hell you may feel like you can forgo any health care insurance, tad risky, but the current system doesn't even give you that choice. The tax system is Marxist, its too big (making it costly), and it is complicated beyond all reasonable means. The shear size and complexity of the system makes it wasteful, hell the only purpose of taxes is to collect revenue, it should not be a works program to create an ever expanding IRS Gestapo, excuse me, I mean bureaucracy.

With the current tax systems high rates and intrusive behavior its also enslaving, for an individuals freedom can be judged in direct proportion to the amount of taxes he must pay. Think that is a far fetched idea, well consider this, every year you work from January till about June just to pay taxes. That sure as hell sounds like slavery to me, forced labor for someone other than the individual performing the labor.

Its bad enough that we allow ourselves to be over taxed, but to make the system complicated, cumbersome, and frustrating is just flat stupid. Oh I can hear the Left Wing Redistributionalists clamoring now, we need the current progressive tax system, it is only fair the rich pay more. You mean to tell me the current system is fair, the progressive tax system is fairest for the rich should pay more? Bullshit Son! So someone who works his ass off 7 days a week, 12 hours a day, should pay more to finance some crack whore in downtown Atlanta? Yeah right, that's real fucking fair, taking what someone else has earned to give to some worthless piece of shit. I would call that stealing.

A flat tax would be so much simpler and cheaper to implement. I personally prefer a flat consumption tax, since that gives me the option of paying or not paying a given tax, but I admit this would be difficult to collect and enforce, (people could pay cash under the table and avoid the tax). But if we didn't waste so much money like we do with the current system maybe we could actually figure out some way to enforce a flat consumption tax. Now a flat income tax would be just as enforceable as the current tax system since we already have an income tax. With the flat income tax April 15th would be history, like Julius Caesar and the Ides of March. A flat tax would result in a much smaller IRS and would free up our reliance on tax accountants and lawyers, which would allow those individuals to spend more time serving much more useful means. Even for the young naive college liberals, who think the government can solve social problems, a simpler more efficient tax system should make sense, cause this would free up more money for whatever tree hugging program it was intended for.

Socialism—centrally planned economy in which the government controls all means of production.

Means of production: Property, Capitol, and Labor.

My Great Uncle Bunyon, my Uncle's Black & Keiser, and I all joined the military at a young age. We were supposedly defending the Constitution, freedom, the hallmarks of capitalism, we were fighting the evils of communism, saving the free world. And we won, the Soviet Union collapsed, we isolated Castro and halted the Gooks at the 38th parallel, yeah we wupped some commie ass! Well, or did we, maybe, don't know, can't tell for sure? Lets see, socialism, centrally planned economy in which the government controls all means of production, (property, capital, labor). Property; are you a homeowner? If you are I bet your paying property tax. Wyoming; the land of wide open spaces, Cowboys, Indians, the heart of the old west, the essence of freedom, yet Uncle Sam owns half the land in the state, HALF! Capital; the heart of capitalism, laizez faire, by god Dudley Uncle Sucker ain't controlling that. Think again Dumbass!! Uncle Asshole has his nasty shit blowed all over that one. The feds control the interest rate, (which is the price of capital), they control the amount of dollars in circulation by controlling the printing press, and they control trading of capitol goods by regulating markets. Need I say more, oh hell yeah, what about labor. If your offering jobs, Uncle Sam is right there to give you advice on who to hire (quotas and other affirmative action legislation), tells you how much to pay them (minimum wage laws), and in some cases tells you how much your employees may work. Here is a general quote from a tree hugging commie liberal, "But those laws are essential for protecting the regular Joe from the Capitalist Pigs". Well Dudley Dumbshit Liberal, Uncle Fucking Sam doesn't stop there, he is right there at the tit of mother labor milking it for all its worth. As I've said before look at your paycheck and see how much the government is taking from your pockets, that is plural "pockets" got to make damn sure no change is left behind. Time for a review there Dudley: socialism—centrally planned economy in which the government controls ALL means of production. Means of production—property, capital, and labor. And just how many of these does the best government money ever bought control, ALL OF THEM! Result = socialism, period.

Its for the kids, as long as its for the kids, nobody wants to see poor little innocent children suffer. These are common slogans for welfare programs, save the kids. HEY DUDLEY!! WAKE THE FUCK-UP!! Welfare trash breeds more welfare trash and you're the one paying for it. Those innocent little snotnosed curtain climbers wind-up being lazy worthless dependant welfare trash just like their piece of shit parents. What about back to work programs? What a crock, the only work welfare creates is Spot-N-Steal work, spot of the day and steal of the night. So not only are your tax dollars going to fund this scum, some of your own direct purchases wind up in the hands of those "innocent" little kids that directly benefit from the welfare system created by your labor.

What about tax breaks for those that have children, that's good right? What? I didn't have the pleasure of creating the little monster, why should I pay for it? If your Catholic neighbor who has the same job as you down at the mill but is against wearing a rubber rain suit and has enough siblings to field a baseball team and gets a huge refund every April 15th and your paying $2500, guess who's indirectly funding the Catholic Church? Well Mr. Martin Luther do you still agree with tax breaks for families with children? Why not give tax relief to prostitutes instead? Tax relief for kids just encourages women to make one man miserable instead of several happy. I would think having children is not exactly good for a woman, shit passing something the size of a bowling ball through your cunt has to be painful, and to top that off you have 18 years of servitude to that bowling ball, at least 18 years. Hell by giving tax relief to prostitutes your killing 2 birds with one stone, 1. your discouraging having kids, meaning less taxes on schools, cops, and prisons 2. you make men happy, a win, win situation!

Another foolish excessive expenditure is the amount we spend on public schooling. If a levy to raise money for the schools is brought to the vote, the Dudley Dumbshit public is sure to pass it, since its "for the kids", "more education is good", "its our future", and other popular help the poor children slogans. WAKE UP you NUMBNUTS! Every dollar you give Uncle Sam to spend on "the kids" is a dollar you can't spend on your own kids, and remember a dollar you spend for your children is a complete dollar, while the natural inherent inefficiency of bureaucracy means just a fraction of that dollar goes to help the kids and a very miniscule amount goes to help your own child, hell in some instances those government programs might end up hurting your child more than helping. And for all the money we spend on education in this country we still trail many nations that spend less when tested against other nations. It's a myth that great amounts of money need to be spent on education at the public level. All that is required is sparking a young minds curiosity. If a student becomes interested in learning, they will seek knowledge of their own free will, and buying new books on a regular basis has very little to do with sparking that interest, shit, no matter how new or old a math book is 2+2 is still 4.

The states biggest encroachment on liberty is a vehicle that far too many fall passionately in line for, War. Yes a free society must defend itself, but during those times quite often valuable liberties are lost all for the sake of National Security. Before supporting a war, consider that your friends, your children, or you may never come back, awful high price for oil.

December 23, 1913 the Federal Reserve act was signed into law. The main objective being to stabilize the monetary system which had experienced a few panics in the 1800's. Damn good thing too, since then we have experienced not just a depression but the "Great Depression", two world wars, stagflation, inflation, and a few recessions. We have seen boom and bust business cycles brought about by expansion of credit handout by this savior of the American economy. Now the Federal Reserve may or may not have been the central cause of these disasters, but I do know that these disasters still occurred (occur), despite the creation of this government panacea to our economic ills. One fact that can not be denied is that the Federal Reserve has put even more control of our lives in the hands of the central authorities in D.C. And the more power you put in control of the federal planners the easier it is for them to drag us into ever broader global crises and conflicts. As each crisis appears the call is for yet more intrusive government. FDIC (Federal Deposit Insurance Company) the guaranteeing of deposits up to a certain amount is another of these government cures, to restore confidence in the banking system. Hell of an idea, leave the bankers free to practice all kinds of dubious schemes, shit no need to worry the feds will bail them out if the shit hits the fan. And from a consumer standpoint no need to differentiate from one bank to the next good ole Uncle Sam guarantees your account up to $100,000. In insurance and financial lingo this is called the Moral Hazard. Moral Hazard defined in insurance as: circumstance which increases the probability of loss because of an applicant's personal habits or morals; for example, if an applicant is a known criminal *(Dictionary of Insurance Terms)*. As I mentioned above in banking this hazard stems from the Federal insurance that allows banks to take risks they probably would not otherwise.

Uncle Sucker guarantees nephew Dudley up to $100,000 on his account but what guarantees does Uncle give nephew of what that $100,000 will buy? The good Uncle need only crank up the printing press and that $100,000 in paper may not be good for anything other than wiping your ass.

This centralized banking creates yet another problem, its centralized. Suppose things are rolling along just fine out in Caliweird (California) I know hard to imagine but bear with me, now suppose there is a drought in Iowa. Well if old Green Jeans in DC decides to lower the rates to help those Sod-busters in Iowa he creates an artificial boom for our Left-coast cousins that eventually leads to inflation. In other words we are not all the same, what's best for me may be disaster for you.

Ever since the Spanish-American War the United States has been on track towards empire. The Civil War signaled the beginning of the end for states rights and Classical liberalism. What makes this all so bad is that we, the average American citizen had the power to prevent it. As bad as the previous statements may seem it is not the worst, the worst is we have the power to reverse this trend, but we have only shifted into high gear. We now have a tax system that takes nearly half our paycheck; there are many forms of slavery and having controlling interest in a mans paycheck qualifies wholeheartedly in my opinion. The monetary system that once relied on the decisions of many bankers and businessmen throughout the country, now relies on the beliefs of an elite minority. The very country that was founded on the fear of big government now has the largest bureaucracy in the history of the world! Seams our fear has become our passion. That which we have become most definitely equals and surpasses what we conquered, King George III.

"I have a notion that usually the great things a man does appear to be great only after we have passed them. When they are at hand they are normal decisions and are done without knowledge. In the case of a General, for example, the almost superhuman knowledge which he is supposed to possess exists only in the mind of his biographer" George S. Patton

8

ELK VALLEY EASE

The following tidbits like an orphan I picked here and there. The words of wisdom that follow contain some philosophy, good old fashioned advice, a touch of humor, and a whole pasture full of bullshit. These short quotes will be broken into three categories; sayings for finance, sayings for government, and the rest will be plugged into a broad category labeled life in general. At the most these are words to live by, at the least something to chuckle at then ignore (leaning heavily on the ignore).

With each quote I will attempt to give its origin, now by origin I mean by what means I first encountered it, not necessarily the original author, although they could be one in the same. I will also give a small explanation of each.

The first category of Isms you may or may not keep at the tip of your tongue but at least keep them close to your wallet. The following words probably won't put you in the mansion on the hill, but should keep you from the box under the bridge.

Having less is having more. Uncle Black

This sounds contradictory, but when it comes to financial independence you will not find a truer statement.

Translation: The less stuff you accumulate the more money you will have, particularly stuff that puts you in debt up to you eyeballs. For example; a two story house, 5 bedrooms, with just 2 rugrats, a dad that's been neutered or (not to be sexist) a mom that's had her cherry cut out.

Plastic surgery. Various, (In other words I don't fucking remember).

Translation: Cutting up your credit card. Yeah, I have heard all the arguments in favor of credit cards, but if you have one of them things you have access to cash you do not have, and you will eventually be using it to buy more stuff, even if you always pay off the charges in time, you wind up spending more money, and saving less. Therefore not having the plastic card is a great money saving device that is self enforcing.

Elk Valley Credit Card. Harry Rich

Translation: Siphon hose. If you have a car on blocks and your truck is on empty, time to break out a piece of hose a siphon some gas out of your wife's broke down clunker. Any purchase prolonged is money saved, besides it guarantees your wife can't get out of the house, leaving money for more important things, like fishing gear and beer.

Its cheaper to pay at the hole. Black

Translation: Get a hooker. Dating girls is an expensive habit; besides you may not get what you want anyway. Think about it, you take a girl out 3 or 4 times before she decides to give up that wonderful stuff, when that money could have been spent the first night getting what you really wanted, therefore leaving the other days for more constructive stuff besides listening to some female yap, and heaven forbid you windup married (talk about expensive). No its much cheaper to just get a hooker, and if Congress would get off their self righteous high horse and legalize prostitution it would be even cheaper.

Speaking of women, what do they have to complain about, hell they have most of the money and all of the pussy.

Translation/meaning: Hell they have complete control over the most desirable commodity known to man, which therefore gives them tremendous access to mans money.

Charity; when it comes to charitable contributions, I give to one fund; the John W. Terry beer fund. Keeping me in good spirits for close to 30 years.

Translation: Self explanatory.

The next category of Ism's will be directed towards that which does so little with so much; government. I'm obviously not an expert on word origins, but the French must have coined that monster called government, how else could it be so fucked up.

Government worker slogan: I ain't afraid of work, I'll lay down right beside it. Keith Wilson

No translation is needed.

Amslak. J.T. Original

Translation: Amtrak. Despite billions in taxpayer funding this outfit is still extremely unreliable. I have had the "pleasure" of riding Amslak on seven short trips from Washington, DC to Manassas, VA, it was on time once, ONCE! Its was late as much as 2 hours, for a 30 mile trip that was supposed to take one hour wound up being three hours. Now I know your thinking 30 miles was scheduled for 1 hour, well if you've ever been to DC, 30 miles in 1 hour is pretty damn good.

Correction to New Deal program W.P.A. (Works Progress Administration); same acronym new name We Piddle Around. Paul Baird

Translation/agency agenda: This agency must be overseeing all government projects; just look at any state sponsored highway grass cutting project. You have one individual pretending to mow, and at least three lookers (I guess their lookers I have no idea what else they could be).

Even a blind squirrel will find an acorn every now and then. Dad

Translation/meaning: Yes every now and then a government project is successful. Big freaking deal, an American League pitcher sometimes gets a base hit in the World Series, but you wouldn't send him up with 2 outs in the bottom of the 9th with the tying run on second.

The last category for this section, Life in General, are quaint little observations I've seen, heard, or experienced down life's highway. Yeah, some may be offensive, then again if you weren't offended by any of the previous pages, I very much doubt I will have any luck in accomplishing that now.

What's the difference between a drunk and an alcoholic? Us drunks ain't got time for those damn meetings. Nate "Bubba" Siltman

Translation: Don't call me an alcoholic! It does not control me, does not prevent me from getting up and going to work, and hell I was even able to quit for a month when the doctor told me my throat was scarred and needed time to heal (well I might have slipped in a day or two of drinking for that month).

If the dog hadn't stopped to shit he'd a caught the rabbit. Dad
If my aunt had balls she would be my Uncle. Clarence "Hippy" Hill
Translation: Don't give me any damn excuses.

When you order the French desert, Peach Pussay, remember Monsieur, don't eata the Peach eata the Pussay. Paul Baird
Translation: Follow proper protocol.

Big woman, big pussy. Little woman, all pussy. Discovered through field tests.
Translation: Logic that does not follow logically, but none the less is still true.

A golf ball and a garden hose; essential practice gear for woman.
Translation: Practice for blow jobs.

Shaking hands with the unemployed. Black
Translation: Taking a piss when your between dates.

Any Who. Kevin Dahl
Translation: The answer to every dilemma.

Its time to make like horseshit and hit the road. Clarence "Hippy" Hill
Translation: Quitting time. Time to hit the road and go home.

The last quote also applies to the current situation, as a lead into for the conclusion of this chapter, its time to wrap it up and move on. If nothing else hopefully this chapter qualified you for a B.S. degree (Bullshit Degree).

9

GO WITH YOUR HEART

Don't lie to yourself, for a cheating heart will tell on you. If something is preventing you from attaining your wants, cease the action, or at least change the direction toward which its aimed. Go with your heart, for if failure then occurs the fault won't be in not trying. When one goes against the hearts desire, then success can still lead to second guessing and the eternal question of, what if.

Areas to be covered considering the hearts desire will be financials, career, politics, and just life in general (No shit, familiar themes, but these things make up economics Dudley). Another theme mentioned before is the need to prioritize, which is absolutely essential here. You will not have the time and/or resources to accomplish all your desires, therefore setting an attainable schedule of priorities is imperative.

Since the title of the chapter is *Go With Your Heart* and I mentioned the need to prioritize your desires I'm going to start with my top priority, finances. Now I obviously covered this earlier, but it is the foremost item on my list, so yes I am going to briefly discuss it again, Dudley's learn by repetition.

When people think of investing, they imagine complicated formula's and cold-hearted investment bankers, believing that one should leave feelings of the heart out of the matter. Nothing could be further from the truth. The cold-hearted, calculated investment decision would say to put all your money in the stock market. But fuck, some folks would die of a heart attack by 30 trying to live with the day to day fluctuations, let alone those occasional bear markets when their portfolio drops by more than 20% in a given year. So obviously the stock market is not for everyone, you must consider your desires and go with your heart, even on financial matters. If you're a riverboat gambler type well stash your winnings in growth stocks, (but have some common sense and don't feed all your stock gains back into your gambling habit). On the other hand if your extremely risk averse, put a high percentage of your money in U.S. treasury securities with small portions elsewhere (e.g., stocks and physical gold).

Desires. If you really want something and are confident its not just a passing whim and have the means to acquire it (legally), by all means do so. Enjoy the fruits of your labor. For example, if you stop by the local Ford dealer gawking at that Mustang GT and have stacks of Mustang magazines, well Dudley park that jewel in your driveway.

Going with the heart, that statement most definitely applies when choosing an occupation. Prioritizing here is extremely important, picking between; money, security, location and shear enjoyment (or less unhappiness, we are talking about work) is no easy task. Now we would all like a six figure salary as a snow plow advisor in Daytona Beach, but it ain't gonna happen. Education; for-crying out loud go to college. I know the younger crowd doesn't know what to major in, well it don't freakin matter, just go you will figure it out along the way. Of course you could join the military and be a U.N. peacekeeper in some third world country full of suicide bombers and ugly women.

You may deem money your top priority when choosing a career (nothing wrong with that, sounds like a winner to me) but if the job you get has a high probability of getting you killed by 35, well shit, it might be good for your widow, but its kinda hard for you to enjoy that money under six feet of dirt. Priorities, Dudley, keep them straight.

We all have certain beliefs, an idea of the way things should be. Here in America one way to express those beliefs is in how we vote. Now when it comes to politics as should be clear by now I am a Classical Liberal, meaning my bare bones thoughts on government are that it only needs to be big enough to keep others from fucking with you and or your property, period. And based on those beliefs I vote Libertarian. Because of this I hear, "How come you 'waste' your vote, it makes no sense to not vote for one of the two major political parties." I hear this shit all the time from people who also say they voted for the lesser of two evils. So your telling me it makes more sense for me to vote for something I don't believe in just because they have a chance to win. Its not a fucking football game, it's a chance for your voice to be heard and if you don't vote for what you believe how in gods name (or anyone else's for that matter) do you expect your voice to be heard. What is this some kind of reverse reasoning by voting for the opposite you believe in, you will get what you want, sounds like some fucked up logic to me (I swear the French must be invading the mind of the American voter, raise a white flag and throw up your hands). Some say you have to be a Pragmatist, bullshit, if we were a land of Pragmatists we'd still be British subjects saying long live the King. At least if I vote for my beliefs whether they have a "chance" to win or not, I know I'll sleep that night with a clear conscience.

Write your liar, I mean Congressman! Keep those pricks on their toes! Now you don't need to do it very often, but at least once a year. It doesn't have to be anything elaborate just make your voice heard (it helps if you mention a specific topic of particular interest to you) and sometimes their office actually reads your letter. For proof hears a couple of letters I wrote to my representative, one of course I got the lousy form letter, but one they actually read and gave a response (the response is included here).

Dear Congressman Wolf:

I am writing to express my disgust at the lack of leadership in Congress since the last Presidential election. Since then Congress has failed miserably at holding the President to his campaign promises and worse they have shirked their sworn duty to uphold and defend the Constitution of the United States.

During the campaign then candidate George W. Bush spoke of free trade, smaller government, less taxes, and he even had the audacity (like most politicians) to speak of the founding fathers even though he apparently never read any more about them than their names. Since his election he has reneged on every one of the above issues, and Congress has not done a damn thing about it.

Allow me to discuss the first of the four campaign issues, free trade. During the campaign when Mr. Bush was asked of about markets, he spoke of opening those markets, and allowing free trade, which would result in not only cheaper products for the American consumer, but also improved products. Have tariffs been lowered? Have quotas been lifted? Of course not, and is anyone in Congress actively pushing the issue, of course not. In fact the opposite has happened. For example an approval of a 30% tariff on primary steel to protect domestic producers was pushed through. What about the domestic producers who use steel as an input for their products, which by the way far outnumber the producers of primary steel, guess what their costs were increased by almost one-third. Result, many of those users of steel are now standing in unemployment lines that are reaching levels not seen in a decade.

Second campaign issue, smaller government. Small? In comparison to what, Dolly Parton's chest? Smaller? With the increase in military spending, taking over of airport security, and the creation of Homeland Security? We already spend more than the next 10 countries combined on National Defense, yet 9/11 still happened. So your answer is turning airport security over to the government. Homeland Security? What the hell is the military for if not national defense? Not to forget that we also have the CIA, INS, and FBI who are supposed to be there to protect our life and liberty. And what has Congress done on this issue, I wish I could say nothing (that would be an improvement over what they actually have done), but no they have drafted most of the legislation that created this bigger government.

Next issue, less taxes. My group single middle class got a $300 refund, gee thanks for giving me enough of MY MONEY to make half a mortgage payment. But oh wait, that "smaller government" has to be paid for some how, whether its through direct tax increases, or indirectly with hidden taxes, (i.e. higher interest rates or inflation), it will have to be paid for.

A brief comment on the reference to our founding fathers referred to earlier. Thomas Jefferson spoke of a wise and frugal government that shall not take from the mouth of labor the bread it has earned, and George Washington mentioned the wisdom of trading freely with other countries but warned of engaging in foreign wars. All of which the President must not have read about, and did Congress call him out? Not no, but hell no!

Now I move on to the failure of our Congressman to uphold the Constitution of the United States, beginning with the introduction of the Patriot Act. This piece of liberty stealing legislation violates the 4th Amendment to the Constitution. This Gestapo like legislation allows the monitoring of Internet usage, which includes emails. Emails; are nothing more than an electronic form of the old-fashioned hand written letter. I do not know what kind of Clintonite definition you all in Congress are using for the word search, but searching through my personal letters is in direct violation of my 4th Amendment rights. The excuse for this legislation is of course national security; apparently our lawmakers have forgot the words of Ben Franklin, "They that can give up essential liberty to obtain a little temporary safety deserve neither liberty nor safety".

Lastly you and your peers have failed to perform their sworn duty as Congressman of the United States. We are currently at war in Iraq, yet no formal declaration of war has been made. As a member of the legislative branch I am sure you are full aware of Article I, Section 8 of the Constitution, that states, Congress shall have Power to declare war. Allowing the President permission to decide on the use of force is not a declaration of war, it's the legislature avoiding to perform their duty. Is Congress trying to pass the blame in case the war goes badly, or is Congress going by way of the Roman Senate as we head towards empire, do they truly believe one man can make a better decision on when to commit our troops to war in a foreign land? If Congress believes our troops should be performing their duty against those people in Iraq, then the least Congress can do over here is perform their duty to the Constitution. I realize that questioning the President's authority and calling for a vote on the war may be unpopular, but an oath is an oath, the young men and women we sent to Iraq are threatened with their life for not honoring their oath. It appears that Congressman see their position as a career that should not be, it's a duty, and that duty includes supporting and defending the Constitution of the United States. I, as a veteran of the Armed Forces also took an oath to the Constitution, but unlike some of my fellow citizens I plan to keep that oath.

I Vote,

John W. Terry

Dear Mr. Terry

Thank you for your recent letter expressing your frustration with what you believe are the failures of Congress in holding the Bush administration to its promises of free trade, smaller government, and less taxes. I appreciate your comments.

I understand that you are disappointed. I support free, but fair trade. I don't believe we should allow preferential trade status for countries such as China which fail to respect the human rights of its people.

I also support an efficient and effective federal government. In that context, Congress and the administration have been faced with unprecedented challenges in responding to the terrorist attacks on America of September 11, 2001, and it takes resources to provide security for all Americans—both at home and abroad. Our world is a dangerous place, and as the president has said, the battlefield is now America. It is important, however, to make sure that those resources are spent wisely as we respond in the aftermath of the terrorist attacks on our country by providing funds for increased homeland security, disaster relief and recovery, counter-terrorism, transportation security and military purposes.

I agree with you that Americans are taxed too much, and I have voted for permanent tax relief which will lower the income tax rate for all Americans and eliminate unfair taxes such the marriage penalty tax and estate tax.

Certainly there is more work to be done on these issues, and I appreciate your taking the time to write and share your views.

Sincerely,

Frank R. Wolf

Although I respect the Congressman's opinion I would like to point out a few fallacies in his response. The fair trade argument which many people use is B.S. Anytime consumers get cheaper goods no matter how, it benefits them buy leaving more dollars in their pockets for other items, and it also gives the foreign country that we trade with dollars to buy American goods. If another country wants to subsidize our consumers so freakin what. "Oh but they will drive Americans out of work with cheaper labor. More bullshit, if this happens how the hell could we afford to trade with those other countries, guess what if we can't afford to buy the Chinese stuff that means we have to produce it here in the good ole U.S. of A, and holy shit that creates jobs. In the mean time if our little yellow friends want to continue giving us all that stuff for nothing more than a piece of paper who cares, sounds like we're living the life of a king to me, enjoy it!

Security for all Americans? Terror attacks rarely happen and the chances are great they won't happen to you. Not all Americans live in New York and DC, those living outside that area should not be forced to pay for the security of those who choose to live in those areas. I would much rather have more money to spend on my own personal security than an overblown bureaucracy like Homeland Security. Instead of increased funds for Homeland Security how about just bringing the troops home.

As for his unfair marriage and estate tax, well, I ain't married and my folks ain't rich. How about helping me, maybe if the tax rate was lower I could afford a wife and/or become rich.

Dear Congressman Wolf,

I was sure glad to see that we paid $820 million dollars to land a golf cart on Mars, by the way thanks for the pictures of the rocks. I'm also happy to know a "fiscally conservative" republican president is considering landing a man on Mars, hell if those spendthrift commie democrats were doing this just think of what they would do, put 2 women there instead, just imagine how much that would cost.

I'm also proud that my tax dollars are helping the "fiscally responsible", heavily neo-con-artist influenced republicans continue to spend billions guarding Saddam in Iraq, while spending millions more on rent-a-cops to sleep while guarding the Washington monument.

I just wonder how often you people in congress stop and realize that money your spending belongs to me and the rest of us taxpayers, or does congress believe that Mr. Inflation (Greenspan) waves his magic wand and creates more wealth.

And now your "fiscally responsible" republican president is proposing a $1.5 billion plan to teach me how to put a ring on some girl's finger. Man I love this idea. About half of those marriages will windup in divorce, costing males like me thousands in lawyer fees and giving some girl we have grown to hate a new house. Hell what's wrong with letting those queers get married, at least when they divorce a male will finally get a house. Oh, but I forgot, that's not the proper thing for a holier than thou "conservative" to do, but spending $1.5 billion in tax payer money on something the church should do is.

I use to vote "conservative" republican,

John Terry

Of course I got the form letter for this.

FIG. 9-1

Picture of mars rock:
—cost 0.82 billion dollars

FIG. 9-2

Picture of earth rock:
—cost 0.082 cents.

The priorities you set forth in the preceding categories should be geared toward what you deem the most important to your overall desires. If all you care about is your own happiness and partying, well you are a brilliant individual, I envy those who can live today with no worry of what tomorrow brings. If your desire is to raise a family (why anyone would want this I don't know, but hey that's your mistake I mean decision not mine) but be prepared to face a lifelong sentence to work like a slave till they lower you down. Now if you believe the key to the hearts desires is summed up by the three real estate maxims, location, location, location, well shit get that hole in the wall high rise in Manhattan or build that shack in the sticks, or at least be working towards that.

If you go the direction your heart tells you, you MIGHT have second thoughts. If you go the opposite direction you WILL have second thoughts. If you truly desire something and it is a viable option, but you choose otherwise, no matter what the outcome you will always wonder what if. If you choose the option of your hearts desires and it succeeds you will be much more satisfied in that endeavor. Of course as humans we will never be completely satisfied, but at least you will be able to move onto another want with no second thoughts.

I have mentioned finances, career, politics, and life in general as if they were means to an end, this may not be so for some, anyone of those could be the summit for a given individual, or a meager start. Hell, then again maybe none of these topics even made your list, but these were not meant to be mutually exclusive, just mere examples or pawns if you will. But one theme mentioned throughout is essential, the need to prioritize. We are only here for a limited amount of time with a limited amount of resources at our disposal, these facts can not be denied.

CONCLUSION

Alright you Dudley Dumbshits, time for a little summary. First here's a statement meant to emanate throughout the preceding pages; stop letting the politically established elite decide what is best for you and allow us the individuals to empower ourselves and make our own decisions. Hell there's a lot more Rednecks in this country than those damned Ivy-League Leaches sitting in some think tank in D.C., its about time the rest of us wake up and fill that tank full of water instead of hot-air.

Now that I clarified the overall theme lets rehash some of the supporting themes. Here's a topic that should be familiar by now; ORGANIZE! It doesn't always need to be some fancy elaborate scheme with spreadsheets and flow diagrams outlining each step along the way, but at least have a purpose, even if the purpose is getting drunk (can't think of one much better, except maybe getting laid).

K.IS.S., speaking of not being elaborate, Keep It Simple Stupid. Do not make things more complicated than they need to be, particularly investing. Besides if your too busy working on some complicated investment formula, you ain't got time for the more important things, like getting drunk and chasing skirt.

Money may be the root of all evil, but desire and scarcity are the seed. The laws of Supply and Demand, all you need to know about Economics.

If you implemented the very complex method of predicting tomorrows weather will be just like today's, you would be more accurate than most the prognosticators on the boob tube, and their supposed to be experts. Now flip the channel over to the business station and here about what all those "experts" on the economy have to say and you know no matter how many times those baboons over at the Federal Reserve fuck with interest rates and the other macro tools in their vaunted tool chest I bet we still have recessions (when are they going to get the hint that their the cause not the cure). DO NOT TRUST THE "EXPERTS"!

I have spoke repeatedly of prioritizing and when it comes to personal investment its importance is amplified, for once again we have a scarce amount of resources (and time) at our disposal and they must be allocated efficiently. And for Crying Out Loud have some sort of Budget. Also keep in mind the need to diversify, in investing diversification is the cheapest and safest form of insurance (and since insurance is like a commodity cheap and safe make it the best). By the way Dudley the secret to increasing your investments is? CUTTING YOUR EXPENSES! Yeah having T-Bones 7 nights a week is nice but having cube steaks on a few nights won't kill you any quicker and contrary to popular belief it isn't necessary to keep up with the Jones's.

Money is the root of all evil, scarcity is the seed, but politicians are the gardeners. Yep, time to rehash the chapter on politics. For decades our fighting men and women put their lives on the line to defeat the evil empire, the Soviet Union. Yet through the ballot box and the crooks on the Potomac we have become the ultimate socialist state. Our highways, schools, medicine, retirement and monetary system are heavily controlled by the government. While on politics let me get one more thing off my chest, the wasted vote Bullshit. Fuck you, to those who criticize me for standing up for what I believe in, and double fuck you to those who believe preachers of the wasted vote B.S. and being chickenshit for not standing behind your true beliefs. The ballot box is the only chance for your voice to be heard if you don't vote for your beliefs how are you going to be heard?

Chapter eight was just some catchy phrases that fall into the different themes stressed throughout the book, and chapter nine topped of the best way to prioritize, go with your heart!

Well I hope I got your attention and maybe even a reaction, like hell yeah! But more likely it was fuck you! If it was the latter, well Dudley, FUCK YOU!

BIBLIOGRAPHY

Graham, Benjamin, and David Dodd. <u>Security Analysis</u>. New York: McGraw-Hill Book Company, Inc., 1963.

http://marsrovers.jpl.nasa.gov/gallery/press/opportunity/20040220a/xpe_Outcr

http://polls.yahoo.com/public/archives/57019568/p-quote-315

http://www.fusinc.com/images/rock_phosphate-3.JPG

http://www.self-go.org/s/es4.htm

Malkiel, Burton G. <u>A Random Walk Down Wall Street</u>. New York: W.W. Norton & Company, Inc., 1996.

Mises, Ludwig von. <u>Human Action</u>. Auburn, Al: Ludwig von Mises Institute, 1998.

Rubin, Harvey W. <u>Dictionary of Insurance Terms</u>. 3rd ed. Hauppauge, NY: Barron's Educational Series, Inc., 1995.

Smith, Adam. <u>An Inquiry Into the Nature and Causes of the Wealth of Nations</u>. Washington: Regnery Publishing, Inc., 1998.

Stokesbury, James L. <u>A Short History of World War II</u>. New York: William Morrow and Company, Inc., 1980.

Studenski, Paul, and Herman E. Krooss. <u>Financial History of the United States</u>. 2nd ed. New York: McGraw-Hill Book Company, Inc., 1963.

www.privacilla.org/government/banksecrecyact.html

You may send comments to:

redneckecon@hotmail.com

0-595-32832-6